DISCARDED

Rescuing the American Dream

Rescuing the
PUBLIC POLICIES

American Dream
AND THE CRISIS IN HOUSING

Rolf Goetze

HOLMES & MEIER PUBLISHERS
NEW YORK • LONDON

First published in the United States of America 1983 by
Holmes & Meier Publishers, Inc.
30 Irving Place
New York, N.Y. 10003

Great Britain:
Holmes & Meier Publishers, Ltd.
131 Trafalgar Road
Greenwich, London SE10 9TX

Copyright © 1983 by Rolf Goetze
All Rights Reserved

Design by Stephanie Barton

Library of Congress Cataloging in Publication Data:
Goetze, Rolf.
    Rescuing the American dream
    Bibliography: p.
    Includes index.
    1. Housing policy—United States. I. Title.
HD7293.G583   1983   363.5'8'0973   82-18748
ISBN 0-8419-0855-9
ISBN 0-8419-0862-1 (pbk.)

Manufactured in the United States of America

Contents

Foreword *by Henry S. Reuss*   ix

Prologue   xi

Acknowledgments   xvii

1   Introduction: *New Housing Realities of the 1980s*   3
    Changes in the Conventional Market   3
    Changes in the Role of Federal Assistance   7
    In Brief   9

2   The Existing Housing Situation: *An Overview*   11
    Overall Changes in the Housing Stock   11
    Mobility, Tenure Patterns, and Housing Costs   14
    Regional Shifts   16
    The Role of Credit   18
    Federal Policies Affecting Housing   23
    How Housing Fundamentals Have Recently Changed   36
    In Conclusion   41

3   Apartments, Homes, and Projects: *In More Detail*   43
    Private Multifamily Rental Housing in Jeopardy   43
    Resident-owned Homes in Changing Market Dynamics   60

  Accessory Apartments and Home Sharing Condominiums and
    Cooperatives: New Tenure Forms 73
  Public and Assisted Multifamily Housing in a Changing
    Context 79
  In Summary 87

4 Federal Actions: *Restructuring the Housing System* 89
  Shifts in Federal Housing Influences 89
  Federal Initiatives to Improve the Local Housing Markets 93
  In Conclusion 98

**5 Local Actions to Improve Housing: *Fitting and
  Fine-Tuning* 101**
  Monitoring Neighborhood Change 102
  Reexamining Public Incentives and Barriers 106
  Dealing with Citizen Expectations and the Media 109
  Applying Assistance More Productively 113

6 Executive Summary: *Two Scenarios* 115
  The Current Realities 116
  The Laissez-faire Scenario 117
  Restructuring Housing Incentives: An Alternative
    Scenario 121

Notes 127

**Appendix A: *Housing Stock Composition by Tenure and
Income, 1978* 131**

**Appendix B: *Federally Chartered Agencies and Direct
Expenditure Programs that Promote Homeownership* 133**

**Appendix C: *Recent Innovations in Home Mortgage
Instruments* 137**

Bibliography 141

Index 145

List of Figures

2.1	Comparison of Households (by Income) and Units (by Gross Monthly Cost) at 25% Cost-Income Ratio, 1978	15
2.2	Federal Housing Programs and Tax Expenditures	28
2.3	Proportions of Home-owner Tax Expenditures by Income Class	34
3.1	The Matrix of Housing Dynamics	63
3.2	The Standard Residential Appraisal Report: FHLMC Form 70	64
3.3	Assistance Strategies for Neighborhood Revitalization	65
3.4	Changes in Suburban Housing Needs with Aging, 1970 to 1980	75
4.1	An Illustrative Savings Program for Home Buyers	98
5.1	A Checklist of Questions for Redirecting Neighborhood Revitalization	107

List of Tables

2.1	1970–1978 National Housing Stock Changes	12
2.2	Federal Housing Programs and Tax Expenditures	26
2.3	Revenue Costs of Home-owner Deductions by Income Class	32
3.1	Various Illustrative Rents for the "Same" Unit	48
3.2	Various Investor Types Owning Multifamily Housing	56
3.3	Local Policy Must Countervail between Extremes	58
3.4	The Golden Mean Diagram: Stabilizing Neighborhood Dynamics	66
3.5	Energy Conservation Incentives and Potential Savings	72
A	Comparison of Households (by Income) and Units (by Monthly Cost) at 25% Cost-Income Ratio, U.S., 1978	131

Foreword

The author suggests that the American housing movement use the Reagan years not to plot a return to a golden age that never was, but to achieve a new synthesis for the post-Reagan era. Goetze does not believe we can generate the effective consumer demand for a construction boom in new housing: new homes are simply unaffordable for increasing numbers of Americans. Instead, there must be more purposeful adaptive reuse of our existing housing.

The stock is there. But too much of it, Goetze believes, is immobilized by intergenerational, interregional, and interclass mismatches.

The older generation uses housing space inefficiently because of badly working tax and credit and alternative housing arrangements.

The older, colder regions have good housing to spare, while the growing sunbelt has fierce housing shortages.

The affluent live in more house than they need, farther from their work and play places than they like, because of out-of-control mortgage interest and real estate income tax deductions. The lower middle class and poor find that their share of the housing supply gets gentrified and converted and they get displaced.

These mismatches, Goetze suggests, could be at least partially corrected. It may be easier to move jobs toward homes than homes toward jobs. It may be easier to devise new housing options for older people than to build a duplicating new town for the young next door. It may be more effective to redirect home owners' tax benefits now concentrated on the affluent to moderate-income people, as West Germany and Canada have done in recent years.

Drawing upon a broad housing experience here and in Europe, and on his eight years as director of housing revitalization in Boston, Dr. Goetze lays out some alternatives worth debating. If alternatives can be achieved, fine-tuning could then occur at the neighborhood level through local policies acting at the margin to match new segments of demand with supply.

The skeptic will reply that all of this is politically impossible. For one thing, Congress subdivides its jurisdiction over cities and housing so that few can see the problem whole. For another thing, those who benefit from the present housing imbalance are not likely to consent to the dissolution of their advantages.

Perhaps. But as we approach the next stage in the history of our cities, we would do well to look at what Goetze has to say.

Henry S. Reuss

Prologue

Housing issues are becoming joined in new ways. This can best be grasped through an illustration. Consider the interplay among four households: Mr. and Ms. Taylor, Mrs. Elliot, the Ryans, and the Smith-Powells (not their actual names):*

In the 1970s the Taylors, a savvy young couple, both of whom were working and renting in Boston, bought with their savings an old southern New Hampshire farmhouse for weekend use. Friday night they would drive up, and on Monday morning they would return to their urban careers. As their earnings mounted, instead of paying off the low-interest mortgage on the farmhouse, they decided in 1980 also to buy in the Boston area, using for half the down payment a loan from Ms. Taylor's father. Rather than buying a $90,000 single-family suburban home, however, they chose a well-worn, six-unit, inner-city apartment building, which the elderly owner, frustrated by rent controls, was willing to "sacrifice" for $90,000 ($15,000 per unit). They improved each unit for sale as a $40,000 condominium, remaking the top unit into a choice penthouse for their own residence. Tax shelters and deductions open to all in higher tax brackets helped them to buy this building—as well as inducing others cheerfully to buy the condos from them at prices that literally gave the Taylors their new penthouse. Since Mr. Taylor is a salesman using his home as a business address, the couple found they could even

---

*Adapted from "The Housing Bubble" by Rolf Goetze, in *Working Papers for a New Society*, January/February 1981. © Trusteeship Institute, 1981.

charge many of the regular carrying costs on their unit—heat, insurance, and utilities—as business expenses.

This fortunate couple is now occupying spaces that formerly would have housed four people in Boston and a family of six in New Hampshire. Those without a grasp of federal tax laws may wonder how they could afford this enviable life-style—unaware that it not only costs them much less than rent for an ordinary dwelling but ultimately also leaves them with title to some "priceless" property. Note how they relied on the savings of others to finance their mortgages.

Nearby, Mrs. Elliott, a widow with grown children, recently sold the family home in the suburbs, netting $40,000, which she planned to invest while moving to a convenient city apartment in a pleasant location. Her tax adviser quickly demonstrated the advantage of buying a condominium instead. First, by reinvesting in the condo, she avoids taxes on the capital gain from the sale of the home. Second, if she invested the $40,000 in stocks, she would realize (say) $4,000 in annual dividend income, which would be taxable. Instead, she pays no tax on the imputed income she gets from her new condominium apartment, and she even gets tax deductions. Finally, as a condominium owner, she will enjoy appreciation of her new investment that is likely to exceed the appreciation she might have enjoyed by investing in stocks. The condo wins hands down.

What clinched it for Mrs. Elliot, however, was the shabbiness of the available rental apartments, contrasted with the proliferation of newly converted condos offered by fine young couples like the Taylors. Oddly, something seemed to be driving all the nicest apartments into condo conversions. So she moved into a dwelling that once housed a large working-class family, even though she won't be using it five months of the year while she is wintering in Florida.

That family, the Ryans, have long been looking for a place to live, and the outlook becomes bleaker all the time. They always had mixed feelings about buying, but it's now a moot choice: the cheapest possible house would require a $7,500 down payment. They don't have anything like that, and there's nobody in the family to lend it. As working, churchgoing people, they reject the prospect of moving into a housing project. Unlike the last time they looked for an apartment in their neighborhood, they find available rentals few and far between and rents out of sight. They heard of one subsidized home-ownership program with a very long waiting list, but they'd prefer to pay their way in their old neighborhood. They wonder what happened to all the $300-a-month apartments.

In the meantime, Mr. Malcolm, a traditional builder with an option on an attractive piece of suburban land, is driven frantic by countless costs—land costs, spiraling material and labor costs, financing and carrying costs—as well as the prospect of dealing with wetlands reviews and zoning appeals that could easily delay him into bankruptcy as he tries to decide whether to build traditional single-family homes, garden apartments, or stylish "planned unit developments" (called PUDs in the trade). He faces so many uncertainties that he finds producing new housing a very discouraging way to earn a living. He was also counting on his financial backer to support him in negotiating the hurdles of building new housing. His banker, however, stung by redlining charges, has shifted his attention to investing in urban revitalization through people like the Taylors and Mrs. Elliot, leaving Mr. Malcolm without financial backing. As it becomes harder and harder to make a living building new housing, Mr. Malcolm is also considering how to shift to the condo conversion business.

For the Smith-Powells, a new two-career couple, it seems impossible to buy in a PUD or anywhere else at this point. Last year they were in a high tax bracket, but currently Mr. Smith-Powell faces an uncertain future as a copywriter on a reduced work week. His wife, a consultant in a special needs program at a local school, knows that her specialty is already being cut back. No lender would extend them credit, so they have modified the basement bar and rec-room of her parents' suburban home, carving out an extra dwelling that affords them some privacy. So far, the neighbors have not objected.

As interest rates ease and housing starts rally a little, some may think the housing crisis is past and that things will be as before. "Back to the city," condo conversions, displacement, and urban revitalization dominated the news for some time—the newsworthy aspects of new settlement patterns of the baby-boom generation. There has, indeed, been a flood tide of new households, both young and old, forming and settling in new ways, but actual patterns are much more complex. Housing prices have become unaffordable, interest rates are still astronomical, and decent rentals seem unobtainable.

"Is the Sun Setting on the American Dream?" and "The 'Hidden Housing Market'—Unused Buildings Become Homes" read more recent headlines. Many builders are now still frustrated not just by the finance roller-coaster but by obsolete practices and regulations, unable to produce or sell appropriate housing to meet the new demands. Other implications of smaller households, like the empty suburban bedrooms left behind by the maturing baby boom, are less generally understood. While the inability to produce enough affordable housing was in the spotlights, new class shifts in settlement patterns and underutilization of much existing housing have become much more important. In the past, moving up into newer housing to raise children in the suburbs safely beyond urban decay seemed everyone's dream. Such frequent moves increasingly separated rich from poor, and owners from tenants; but these patterns no longer dominate.

New life-styles now combine with changing economic forces to bring forth unanticipated residential patterns. Competition for existing housing has entered urban neighborhoods that only a few years ago seemed headed for oblivion. Households pioneering this urban rediscovery encounter the previous residents still there and ambivalent about "gentrification." The newcomers see fresh opportunities and new challenges, while those who have hung on so long are often mistrustful, regarding the newcomers as simply still another threat to be countered in their fight to survive. Absentee owners eagerly sell, profiting from market change.

The purpose of this book is to broadly identify the new forces already reshaping urban neighborhoods, trace their linkages, and point out opportunities in revitalization that are advantageous to both newcomers as well as previous residents if we take a fresh approach. The intended audience includes all who have a stake in urban housing: residents, owners, managers, investors, buyers and sellers, activists and conservationists, along with the traditional planners, politicians, and policy makers.

This presentation is a reconnaissance, not of uncharted territory, but rather of new realities and perceptions, easily overlooked or underestimated in importance.

The older generation that blesses the thermostat that controls the central heating every morning is confounded by the young who reintroduce into living quarters the wood stove with its smoke and ashes. Similarly, suburban parents are puzzled as their offspring seek out tired and worn multifamily structures with tenants to build their new communities. Will this be a significant and lasting new pattern?

Data on these changes are very imperfect. Even the 1980 U.S. census does not make the extent of coming changes much clearer. Those who demand definitive statistics will never be satisfied before the opportunities for timely actions have passed. But it is already becoming clear that around 1975 the excess of supply over demand reversed in many areas. The urban policy tools fashioned to deal with blight are not only inadequate but often inappropriate to handle the rising competition for urban space between those who ask for simple shelter and those for whom scarce housing is now both a tax shelter and an inflation hedge. Because there are no better data, the analysis here is partly based on inferences drawn from many instances of households everywhere coping with these new situations. Along the way it sheds some light on a host of imponderables: What governs the likely extent of urban revitalization? What is the nature of the rental housing crisis? Is home ownership now so favored by federal income tax breaks that much rental housing will be converted to condominiums and thereby "saved"? Are home owners receiving windfalls, or are their tax deductions simply driving up inflation, home prices, and mortgage interest rates? What are the current and potential roles of direct federal assistance? And how significant are the indirect public policy influences on urban revitalization?

This book attempts a coherent synthesis of the many separate underlying strands obscured by such new urban buzzwords as redlining, greenlining, gentrification, displacement, unaffordability, and community control. Chapter 1 is an introduction; Chapter 2 is a descriptive overview of the housing situation. Chapter 3 provides a more detailed analysis of changes in the four main components of our existing housing—apartments, homes, condominiums and cooperatives, and assisted projects. Chapter 4 ventures into prescription, suggesting potential federal initiatives for restructuring the local housing market system to reduce inequities. Chapter 5 suggests new local initiatives to help communities cope with changed realities. Chapter 6 provides two contrasting scenarios to summarize the insights developed throughout this book.

Widening differences between haves and have-nots competing for the same housing stock threaten to generate counterproductive clashes. To avert them requires a deeper grasp of the emerging situation. Political changes under way in Washington provide the opportunity to reflect on past urban assistance programs and to reconsider what policies are most appropriate to the new realities.

Acknowledgments

Many helped in this reconnaissance of the changing housing prospect. First and foremost, the undertaking would not have been possible without the generous support of the Ford Foundation and the encouragement of Lou Winnick, who suggested that I try linking all these housing strands together. Three readers of the completed first draft should be singled out for their penetrating questions, challenges, and suggestions: Tom Chmura of SRI-International, Jim Wallace of the President's Commission on Housing, and Konrad Perlman of the Department of Housing and Community Development of Washington, D.C.

Colleagues in diverse fields shared ideas and helped in various ways. Bob Kuttner's grasp of the broader issues often guided me. Saul Shiefman helped confirm new housing patterns and trends. To gain perspective about them, Donna Sorkin of Public Technology, Inc., and her network of peers in major cities linked by the Urban Consortium were invaluable. Langley Keyes and his MIT students raised provocative points. Allan Groves enabled me to understand some lenders' viewpoints, George Slye revealed effects on the real estate industry, and Pat Hare helped me grasp new aspects of the accessory apartment issue.

"Neighborhood listening" as a concept may have been coined by Bob Engler. In any case, colleagues at Stockard & Engler joined me in New Haven in trying out some of these new approaches to local policy formulation, and Mary Lou Skerritt suggested how practicing planners should be addressed on these issues. Cushing Dolbeare of the Low Income Housing

Information Service, Charles C. Cook of the Lincoln Institute of Land Policy, and Kent Colton, recently staff director of the President's Housing Commission, provided many welcome opportunities to sort out these ideas.

In all this my wife, Julie Anne, once again not only put up with the household pressures raised by "doing another book" but cheerfully typed drafts, debated points, and suggested edits.

Reviewing my initial outline, the late Fred Vogelsang, editor of the *Journal of Housing*, encouraged me by calling it an "ambitious but worthwhile undertaking." I did not realize then how ambitious—and you, the reader, can now judge how worthwhile. Already I feel aware of shortcomings for which I accept full responsibility. We are in the midst of unprecedented housing changes. Rather than wait for the dust to settle, I think it important to publish now to help inform debate while there is still time for us to influence the outcomes.

Belmont, Massachusetts
March 1983

Rescuing the American Dream

Introduction

NEW HOUSING REALITIES OF THE 1980s

In 1977 I wrote:

Tsunami accounts describe how a tidal wave first pulls the waters way back, exposing the hidden ocean floor, before rushing in and swamping everything in sight. Today we are puzzled exploring the mysterious ocean floor and arguing about questions of neighborhood blight, lack of mortgage credit, and dwindling city revenues. When the tidal wave of new households engulfs urban areas, most of the existing housing supply will be brought into play because the nation simply cannot produce enough new housing in the next fifteen or twenty years to meet the new demand.[1]

Only five years later there is, indeed, a sharp contrast between the housing prospect then and now; excess supply has given way to excess demand. Demographic changes, the so-called baby-boom generation reaching the age of settling down, are only the most visible aspects. Through the early 1970s the image of traditional families settling in suburbia persisted. Meanwhile, cities spurred by the government's Great Society programs were still striving to rebuild blighted areas with assisted projects, unaware that lack of enough housing demand, both in household numbers as well as income, had contributed to urban blight. Public attitudes and perceptions about housing are sharply at variance with reality.

CHANGES IN THE CONVENTIONAL MARKET

Now the supply-demand imbalance has suddenly reversed, and new construction has become bogged down in red tape and soaring building costs. In the face of housing-demand shifts and federal assistance cutbacks, enough new construction in the right places often seems unattainable. Here housing is no longer to be disinvested as a "throwaway" consumer good but is suddenly a prized commodity. Less visibly, the urban employment base also became transformed. As urban blue-collar manufacturing waned, services and information processing involving white-collar workers rose to dominance in central cities.

One might have assumed that classes living separately would simply continue to commute daily past one another, the blue collars outward to the new industrial parks, and the professionals inward to the center city, leaving families behind in various bedroom suburbs with their schools, yards, fresh air, and sunshine. Energy shocks and inflation began to change this, however, as the rising cost of commuting in both time and money hit home. Many in the baby-boom generation formed two-career households and postponed having children until they had first bought a home. With less emphasis on child-raising, people began approaching their housing choices in new ways, and many more than before began buying in urban areas.

Inflation introduced some important changes in the housing prospect with subtle but long-ranging consequences. Americans have always sought to own their homes, but in the past fifteen years, inflation and the fixed-rate mortgage enhanced home ownership excessively, compounding the baby-boom housing demand. During this period, the American economic system, acting through advertising, tax laws, and rising consumer expectations, encouraged more and more living on credit. Interest paid by consumers on anything from charge-card purchases to homes is not only paid with dollars cheapened by inflation but is also tax deductible. Conversely, interest earned on savings is taxed. As a result, savings erode during inflation, but money tied up in a home is tax sheltered. As households rose into higher tax brackets, they were widely advised by financial experts to assume more debt to reduce their federal income tax burden.

Buyers who acquired homes between 1965 and 1978, when fixed-rate 6–10-percent mortgages were common, discovered after a few years that home ownership was not only *not* costing them anything, it was actually rewarding them substantially. When mortgages were 3 percent above the inflation rate, as they traditionally were before the mid-1960s, people had always stressed home ownership as a forced savings account by which owners built up equity as they amortized their mortgages. However, the fixed mortgage interest rate turned out unexpectedly to be well below the rate of inflation, producing phenomenal returns on equity.

The average home in this period appreciated faster than the nominal interest rate on its mortgage. To buy a $30,000 home in 1970 a family could put down $6,000 and pay $186 monthly until 1990. By 1980 this house was already worth well over $80,000 almost anywhere and possibly much more if located in a supercharged market context like California. The owner, scheduled to continue fixed payments on his 7-percent, $24,000 mortgage for another ten years, is also paying off his obligation in dollars shrunken by inflation. He is thus reaping a double advantage from the inflating economy. Income tax deductions for mortgage interest and local property taxes only served to further convince him that home ownership was the best bargain he ever made, as he readily explained to any and all who would listen.

Those entering into home ownership later in the 1970s found home prices higher and the fixed interest rate on their mortgage a little more breathtaking—11 or 12 percent—but "tax bracket creep" had also moved them into higher income tax brackets, offsetting to some degree their higher borrowing costs. Since housing continued to appreciate more rapidly, home ownership made sense to them. These prospective buyers often heard from those who bought earlier that their mortgages at 9 percent had also seemed high to them at the time. So as the mortgage rates continued to move on up, the new buyers in turn also became vociferous advocates of home ownership. The first rung on this ladder of opportunity simply seemed somewhat higher.

Some home buyers, especially affluent two-career households, shrewdly chose underpriced urban dwellings, convenient to their work, which appreciated even more rapidly. The $40,000 row house in Boston's South End bought for $15,000 down was not unusual. After the owner invested an additional $35,000 plus much evening and weekend time, it was sold two and one-half years later for $180,000 as three $60,000 condominiums, more than tripling the owner's investment. Clearing $130,000 in thirty months, this owner profited much more from his housing than he was able to earn at work during the same period.

Media coverage, cocktail conversations, and even in-flight magazines persuaded ever more people to sacrifice to attain home ownership. Two careers and forgoing children became an accepted part of the route to the American dream of a home of one's own. People spent much more on buying a house than they would ever have dreamt of paying in rent, because the belief took hold that, even in spite of the current price of entry, owning a home was too good an investment to pass up. Few realized that thanks for these windfalls were due to banks for issuing below-market fixed rate mortgages, as well as countless savers who had been shortchanged for years. Most rhetoric asserted that such mortgage terms are still an American "right." Savers, however, have withdrawn more and more of their money and found access to better investments like Treasury bills and money market funds.

Some countervailing trends have already developed from side effects of these changes. "Every year one family in five moves" was accepted as the norm for years. Tenants were always the more mobile, but they are now discouraged by tight housing and much higher rents encountered upon moving.

Many home owners with favorable mortgages have also become locked in to their properties, because by moving they lose the benefits of holding a below-market mortgage. Inflation induces more home owners to stay put, breaking past patterns of paying off mortgages early. Until the early 1970s many home owners, especially those of ethnic and working-class backgrounds, would still strive to pay off their mortgage. Buyers traditionally sought to avoid having a prepayment penalty clause in their mortgage. The more affluent, being in higher tax brackets, were the first to realize the advantages of holding on to a favorable mortgage and using their savings to expand the home or to acquire second or even third homes. Many shrewdly became mortgaged to the hilt. Altogether, as lenders granted twenty-five- and thirty-year mortgages and supply and demand in credit became unbalanced in the 1970s, an unprecedented amount of capital became tied up in housing, driving up interest rates.

Belatedly, lenders sought to devise incentives to encourage people to retire their mortgages early, but these were largely futile. Even the "due upon sale" clause in many mortgages proved unenforceable. At the same time, along with the general public, lenders consistently underestimated the future rate of inflation in setting the terms on all new mortgages. As a result, many lenders' portfolios of residential mortgages are yielding them a return of under 10 percent. Had passbook savers continued to leave their savings in these banks, this would be no problem. However, 5 or 6 percent interest seems too little when savers can safely get much more elsewhere. Lenders have had to pay more and more to keep savers from transferring their savings to money market funds, paying as high as 16 percent at times. To extricate themselves now from this so-called inverse yield predicament (earning less than they have to pay to attract savings), lenders are trying a host of new measures including innovative variable rate and much higher interest mortgages, and sharing with the home buyer in the appreciation. Many more are becoming mortgage brokers as they look to the secondary market and tax-exempt notes as well as to pension funds for new sources of credit to loan out to tomorrow's home buyers. Lenders are now determined not to be caught off base again, holding fixed long-term commitments themselves. However, a 14 percent variable-rate mortgage is much less attractive to the home buyer than even the 14 percent fixed-rate mortgage his friend obtained only recently. In many areas this has stopped conventional housing market turnover and induced sellers and brokers to invent "creative financing."

This fundamental lending shift toward indexed mortgages eliminates one of the factors that spurred housing inflation: cheap mortgages. To those now seeking to buy homes, however, it seems very unfair that they are asked to pay for the windfalls already reaped by those who bought their homes years ago. Few realize that the home-owner windfall mortgage was an anomaly that made housing an extraordinary investment in the past fifteen years—one that could not continue. Many will angrily stay put, expecting the government to reduce inflation or at least provide better mortgage terms, while some devise their own credit arrangements directly with sellers.

CHANGES IN THE ROLE OF FEDERAL ASSISTANCE

The direct federal role in housing has also changed in a decade and this, too, has many complex dimensions that are only summarized here. Through the mid-1970s there were an unprecedented number of housing starts as the nation attempted to "produce" its way out of its housing problems. An increasing part of these starts were developments publicly assisted through federal mortgage insurance and subsidies—and often state tax-exempt bonds as well. The growing dependence on government assistance and the inflationary impact of government regulations on housing production costs were not generally recognized. Complete rehabilitation in place of stable maintenance was also encouraged through tax provisions like accelerated depreciation, without awareness that this would force turnover sales later, at a time when mortgage interest rates rose sky-high.

Government-insured and -subsidized financing raised general housing standards but also inflated production costs and overall housing expectations. Nevertheless, reliance on increasing amounts of assistance continued, even as evidence was surfacing that many assisted developments were flawed and not financially viable. Produced and operated independently of the market, they lacked effective cost controls. An early warning of possible retreat in the federal housing commitment was signaled in 1975 by the consolidated community block grant and Section 8 housing assistance programs initiated under President Ford. Although these programs reduced some of the red tape associated with the previous categorical programs, they promised ever more, yet were not backed by adequate financial commitments. In successive years, resource commitments began to taper down at the same time that per-unit production costs soared. These programs raised expectations even as actual production volume dwindled. The Section 8 assistance falsely promised to add to the stock and also to save many from displacement, when in fact it was increasingly being channeled to bail out already-built subsidized developments in financial trouble to avert their loss.

Since the election of President Reagan, the federal commitment to assist housing directly has been visibly cut back, dashing the expectations and threatening the livelihood of all who had come to depend on more and more government assistance. Much of this was inevitable because the system had become so overextended. Few felt Section 8 was perfect, but most felt it was better than nothing. However, it seems likely that there will now be little more assisted new construction, because the limited funds will be needed to save assisted housing already built. The private market is not likely again to pick up the slack in new production either, because development is fraught with more costly uncertainties and red tape. The 1980s promise thereby to become the decade of adaptive reuse of existing stock, financed not through federal government assistance but through local initiatives taking advantage of tax provisions. Substantial new housing construction in the 1980s thus seems unlikely to alter prospective housing shortages significantly. Most accommodation will have to occur under roofs that already provide shelter.

The long-term trend toward smaller household size went virtually unnoticed in the 1970s. More elderly and more offspring, rather than live with others, came to head their own households in the 1970s. In many cities, dwelling counts increased even as population declined, confusing the public. Boston, for example, changed from 640,000 persons in 232,000 dwellings in 1970 to less than 580,000 persons in 240,000 dwellings in 1980. The number of persons per dwelling dropped from 2.76 to less than 2.4—a 13 percent drop. Now, as fewer leave home, this long-term trend may slow or even reverse.

This underutilization of housing—that is, using it at less than previous capacity—will change during the 1980s as more people reach the conclusion that they cannot afford to live so "spread out." The carrying costs to buy, maintain, heat, manage, and upgrade housing have risen phenomenally. At the same time the expectations of future gains, of more appreciation and further profiting from inflation, have diminished. More income is needed now to meet current costs. A single elderly widow remaining alone in the family home and couples involved in marital separation will find that they can no longer afford so much space. In addition to more doubling up, more smaller units will be fashioned in new ways within existing structures. Legally or otherwise, people are installing what are variously referred to as "in-law," "ancillary," or "accessory" apartments in formerly single-family residences. Even "granny flats," new quarters added on to existing lots, are being mentioned. Single and two-person households may have their own semiprivate spaces in attics, basements, or even in arrangements not unlike maids' quarters in a previous era. There may not yet be widely recognized names for these new accommodations, or even legal recognition of their existence, but these conversions have been going on for some time in strong market areas favorable to new life-styles. As shortages induce more adaptive reuse, necessity will spur the rejuvenation of much existing housing in this decade. A preview of this future could already be glimpsed in the 1970s in student areas with their basement apartments and greater diversity of shops and activities, or in popular resort areas where every square foot of shelter is valuable and in demand. The dominant issue here is not displacement, but adaptively devising ways of doing better with less resources, less waste of space.

The challenge to the public sector in this decade is to help demand match supply, facilitate creative market adaptations, and not stand in the way. This overview has already suggested that past publicly regulated lending practices and federal tax and assistance policies have exacerbated problems, unbalancing both housing and credit markets. As a result of such man-made obstacles, the urban revitalization process so far has proceeded very unevenly and often inequitably. In too many ways feast seems juxtaposed with famine, as one street gentrifies while problems fester nearby. As a more detailed look at the dynamics of separate components of the existing stock will reveal, public policies should balance things out and help local interests countervail against market extremes.

Out-of-place policies regarding lending, taxes, and assistance have inadvertently become part of the problem, encouraging the Haves to profit by taking over more housing, leaving less for the disadvantaged. There is no longer even the promise of enough government assistance for the disadvantaged. Everyone is asked to pay much more for mortgages now. However, the more affluent can continue to take increasing tax deductions that in effect substantially reduce their mortgage costs. The better off one is, the greater this housing subsidy will be. The principal remaining federal housing support, the home-owner deduction, is very disruptive wherever housing shortages induce speculation and the affluent exploit their advantage over more moderate income tenants.

IN BRIEF

Tax provisions interact with local zoning and building codes to produce speculation in many areas instead of needed housing. Federal tax incentives have made well-built but recently neglected and overlooked existing housing a far better investment than new construction—even in areas where builders are not hampered by too many regulations. New development has become unaffordable not only because wages, prices for materials, and land and financing costs have soared, but also because demand is greatest in built-up areas, where community opposition and costly delays easily confront any large scale redevelopment.

For years experts warned of an impending housing shortage as new starts faltered. Wherever a serious shortage has emerged, strong demand raised the prices of whatever housing became available. In the longer run it is unlikely that property values can be sustained at much more than three times resident income, suggesting either that price increases must moderate or that those now entering the housing system will settle for less housing.

Despite increased financing costs, tremendous appreciation of existing residential real estate occurred over the last decade. Combined with the federal tax benefits associated with ownership, this encouraged a "buy now" psychology, particularly among the more affluent, two-career households. Home-owner tax deductions open to households in the higher tax brackets reduce their mortgage interest rates significantly: A 13 percent mortgage still "costs" a two-career household in the 50 percent tax bracket under 7 percent, below the rate of inflation. Where desirable new stock is unavailable, this demand turns to existing stock. Accordingly, middle-income, first-time home buyers are shifting demand from unaffordable single-family, suburban property to condominiums and to housing located in lower-income neighborhoods.

Coordinated national and local leadership is required to address longer-range issues posed by the ways this bias in the federal income tax code interacts with local regulations. Home-owner deductions in effect create special tax shelters for the affluent that divert resources from other sectors of the economy. These are economically inefficient when they produce excessive gains for owners of existing housing instead of new housing.

Since we now seem unable to build enough new housing in high-demand areas, more creative uses for the existing urban stock are bound to develop. Much better use of the shelter already there is possible. In fifteen years we have come a long way from thinking we could simply demolish and outbuild blight. Fifteen years ago some people thought urban renewal was a government program to bring the middle class back to the cities, while others were sure they would never come back. Now, younger middle-class households are choosing urban areas without direct government assistance. The fixed interest rate mortgage may have fostered this urban resurgence, but housing shortages will persist for some time in many areas, favoring continued urban revitalization. We have a unique opportunity to influence these creative forces of fix-up and revitalization. Like any other strong forces, they must be understood to avoid backlashes, acrimony, or more destruction and waste of existing housing. To these ends it is appropriate to examine the existing housing situation more closely.

The Existing Housing Situation
AN OVERVIEW 2

OVERALL CHANGES IN THE HOUSING STOCK

The *Annual Housing Survey (AHS)* is the broadly accepted yardstick for detecting changes in the housing stock between 1970 and 1978. It provides only limited insights into recent changes in the national housing situation and many people differ with its particulars, but we have no better overall statistics. The following inferences are drawn from table 2.1, which summarizes data in the 1978 *AHS*.

From 1970 to 1978 the national housing stock increased by 22 percent, to 82.8 million year-round housing units. Vacancies increased, however, by one-third, to 5.7 million units, so in 1978 there were 77.2 million occupied dwellings.

The basic mix of types of structures in the stock did not substantially change in the 1970s in spite of the fact that 16.4 million dwellings, one in five, were new. Of the total 1978 stock 55.5 million units (67 percent) were single-family dwellings, 23.6 million (27 percent) were in multifamily structures, and 3.7 million (5 percent) were mobile homes.

Looked at in tenure terms, in 1978, 50.3 million units (over 65 percent of the occupied stock) were resident owned and 26.9 million were rented out. Over 90 percent of the rental stock was completely private. The *AHS* shows that only 1.9 million dwellings (7 percent) were in housing projects, and another 0.7 million (about 2½ percent) were under government rent subsidies. Others suggest the number of assisted units is lower. In any case, this portion is not likely to grow substantially.

Condominiums and cooperatives, so often discussed but virtually

TABLE 2.1
1970–1978 National Housing Stock Changes

(dwelling units in millions)

	Total 1970	Total 1978	Inside SMSAs in central cities 1970	Inside SMSAs in central cities 1978	Inside SMSAs not in central cities 1970	Inside SMSAs not in central cities 1978	Outside SMSAs 1970	Outside SMSAs 1978
All-year-round housing units	67.7	82.8	22.6	25.2	23.5	30.9	21.6	26.8
Total Δ, year-round housing units, 1970–1978		+15.1		+2.6		+7.4		+5.2
Total built after 4/70		16.4		3.2		7.3		5.8
Vacant year-round housing units	4.3	5.7	1.2	1.7	1.0	1.6	2.0	2.3
Total occupied housing units	63.4	77.2	21.4	23.4	22.5	29.3	19.6	24.4
Total occupied stock Δ, 1970–1978		+13.8		+2.0		+6.8		+4.8
Owner-occupied housing units	39.9	50.3	10.3	11.6	15.8	20.8	13.8	17.9
Mobile homes + trailers	1.8	3.0	0.2	0.1	0.7	1.2	1.0	1.7
1 unit in structure	35.5	44.0	8.7	9.8	14.4	18.4	12.4	15.8
2 to 4 units in structure	2.2	2.3	1.1	1.2	0.6	0.8	0.4	0.4
5 or more units in structure	0.5	0.9	0.3	0.5	0.1	0.4	0.1	0.1
Stock Δ, 1970–1978		+10.4		+1.3		−5.0		+4.1
Stock built after 4/70		10.6		1.3		4.8		4.4
Renter-occupied housing units	23.6	26.9	11.1	11.8	6.7	8.5	5.8	6.6
Mobile homes + trailers	0.3	0.6	—	—	0.1	0.2	0.2	0.4
1 unit in structure	8.5	8.3	2.3	2.1	2.6	2.6	3.7	3.5
2 to 4 units in structure	6.2	7.4	3.3	3.7	1.7	2.2	1.2	1.5
5 or more units in structure	8.5	10.5	5.5	6.0	2.3	3.5	0.7	1.1
Stock Δ, 1970–1978		+3.3		+.7		+1.8		+.8
Built after 4/70		4.6		1.6		2.1		0.9

SOURCE: Prepared by R. Goetze from 1978 *Annual Housing Survey*, Parts A and C
NOTE: Δ = Net change. SMSA = Standard Metropolitan Statistical Area

nonexistent in 1970, had rapidly increased to 1.2 million units in 1978 but were still under 2 percent of the occupied stock. They surely have continued to grow since then. The *AHS* reveals little about them. One cannot tell how many are newly built, how many are conversions, how many are rented out.

The 13.8 million net stock increase from 1970 to 1978 resulted from 15.2 million new units built after April 1970 and 1.4 million units lost. The losses were virtually all older rentals, but one cannot tell whether they were demolished or converted to owner occupancy.

Of the units added after 1970, 10.6 million dwellings (70 percent)

FIGURE 2.1
Comparison of Households (by Income) and Units (by Gross Monthly Cost) at 25% Cost–Income Ratio, 1978

(in millions of households or units)

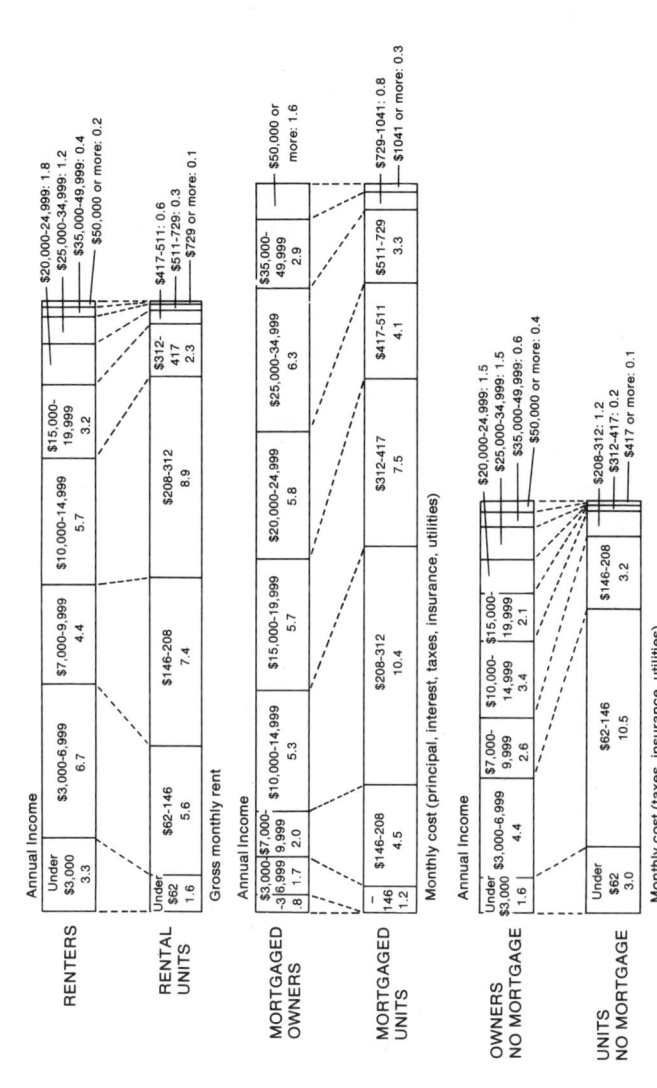

SOURCE: Derived from 1978 Annual Housing Survey, Vol. C, Table A-1. Prepared by Low Income Housing Information Service.

presents a hypothetical matching of households by annual income with dwelling units by monthly housing costs, developed by the LIHC from the 1978 *AHS*.

There were only 7.2 million rental units under $146 per month, which is all the 10 million renter households under $7,000 could "afford" spending no more than 25 percent of income on housing. This reveals either a "deficit" of at least 2.8 million affordable rentals, or the fact that millions of lower income tenants must have been spending well over one-quarter of their income on housing in 1978. At $10,000 income, $208 monthly, supply and demand balanced out. However, rents have since risen more rapidly than rental incomes and will continue to do so, worsening the plight of tenants.

In contrast, there were 16.6 million homes costing less than $208 monthly alongside the 8.6 million home owners under $10,000 without a mortgage in figure 2.1. Even for the 4.5 million resident owners under $10,000 *with* mortgages, there were 5.7 million dwellings for less than $208 a month. Examined this way, the *AHS* data confirm the incentives for staying put and owning your own housing.

When faced by such statistics, many people allow their eyes to glaze over; others seek to challenge details as if this could alter the big picture. In any case, the implications and political import of figure 2.1—the worsening picture for tenants and tomorrow's home buyers—are hard to develop in dramatic form from such statistics even if they were more detailed and up to date. All too easily we debate dry statistics while allowing situations to worsen until more dramatic evidence of problems surfaces, like rent strikes or illegal conversions.

REGIONAL SHIFTS

Residential shifts between regions are even more difficult to present in such statistical terms. Nevertheless, they are critically important because such housing shifts magnify underlying problems and shape so many local housing actions. Because suitable data are not yet at hand, the following discussion lays out the issues conceptually, for confirmation in the future as better data become available.

In many places, particularly some urban neighborhoods, the excess of supply over demand of the early 1970s seems suddenly reversed into a housing crunch—a situation in which people *feel* there is not enough housing to go around. In weak areas this has happened only here and there, but in strong markets, like the San Francisco Bay area or around Washington, D.C., it seems to have completely transformed the housing outlook throughout the region. The introductory chapter suggested that post-Vietnam inflation compounded the impact of the baby-boom housing demand by temporarily but sharply enhancing owner-occupied housing as an investment through windfall home-owner mortgages.

In housing, supply and demand mismatches do not even out rapidly; imbalances persist for years. Over two decades ago, suburban demand went up and inner-city demand declined. In 1970, the same house model in the city was simply worth considerably less. More recently, and consequently less integrated into our thinking, there have been bigger migrations away from regions of decline toward growth, from the Northeast toward the South and West. So in the 1980s, the same house model in the Southwest is simply worth considerably more. These macrodifferences between regions compound with the local divergences in housing values.

Statistics cannot yet convey the sharp differences that selective migrations have wrought on local population composition. Growing regions attracted people in their twenties and thirties, leaving a corresponding deficit in the areas from which they came. "Go-getters," a major asset to any economic base, tend to be among the movers, draining both brain and brawn from weaker areas. Whether laborers or lawyers, those beginning their jobs and careers tend to work for less compensation than those already established and staying behind. This suggests there is a productivity multiplier magnifying the impact of population differences between growth and mature areas.

The more affluent and adventurous "empty-nesters," and retirees freed from family and job ties, also became increasingly mobile, moving out to new areas. This creates a secondary deficit, further drawing down the mature skills and civic commitment in areas they left behind. Such significant changes in population composition overshadow total gains or losses in population.

Media contrasts between Detroit and Houston, for example, now amplify such differences, in effect undermining local confidence in declining areas by stressing problems and boosting growth in already-growing areas. This not only furthers more migration, but also affects the morale and expectations of the rooted residents. In 1970, an urban college graduate had to be prepared to defend living in the city. Today, moving to a declining city similarly calls for a thicker skin.

The enormous implications of these demographic changes will be surfacing for years. To see how these factors affect local situations, consider jobs, housing, and lending.

In terms of jobs, growth naturally brings many more opportunities. Offices, manufacturing plants, as well as residences, must be built, occupied, and supplied with services. Roads, utility systems, and transportation networks are needed, and all of these translate into lots of new jobs. In declining areas, lack of private sector expansion makes the established labor force much more watchful to see that its living standards do not erode. Benefits and work rules become preoccupations.

In housing, the contrasts between regions seem most baffling. In growing areas where it seems not enough new housing can be built, values of existing structures have soared. A home in California can cost three times as much as a similar house in Ohio. Demand-supply mismatches thus translate into large differences in housing costs and perceived local well-being.

The Californian buys a home as an investment, counting on the 20 percent housing appreciation to continue, and relying on personal income tax deductions to continue to result in a negative real mortgage interest rate. As long as one remains employed and in a high tax bracket, one's venture pays off handsomely.

In Ohio, many a home buyer feels that this mortgage interest rate is too high, and most bankers concur because the owner may become unemployed or the home may fail to appreciate. In Ohio, selling the house in case of default would be difficult. Local bankers thus seek federal insurance for local loans and prefer to invest their depositors' money in the secondary market, thereby furnishing still more of the capital that areas like California seek.

Uniform national lending policies here illustrate unforeseen local effects. In the 1960s, California banks paid more interest and charged higher mortgage rates than elsewhere. However, the national secondary mortgage market encouraged more capital to flow to such growth areas, fueling housing inflation where growth controls prevented developments to match demand.

Complexity obscured the underlying causes of the situation. Nevertheless, people turned expectantly to government to mend matters wherever local expectations were not met. Not enough decent housing? Not enough jobs? Inadequate or unaffordable lending? In the ensuing policy debate, underlying factors, such as changing demography, mobility, and the cause and effects of demand-supply mismatches, were overlooked. Local efforts were directed at creating highly visible jobs, housing, or loan programs that often supplanted private action.

THE ROLE OF CREDIT

Most home mortgages in the United States since the Depression were provided by thrift institutions, generally called savings banks. These matched up savings in many small individual accounts (which depositors could withdraw at will) with twenty-year, fixed-interest mortgage commitments to home buyers. Savings banks paid up to 5 percent for savings and charged 1–1½ percent more on mortgages, living on the difference. The average mortgage typically lasted only eight years as home owners "filtered up" to newer, better homes or owners paid them off. The volume of savings also grew more or less steadily and predictably—before post-Vietnam inflation. Linking short-term deposits with long-term, fixed-interest lending commitments caused little concern in the 1960s. In fact, federal Regulation Q, which allowed savings banks to pay up to 5¼ percent but no more to depositors (¼ percent more than commercial banks), was intended to preserve this home mortgage system.

Unfamiliar Patterns Since the Mid-1960s

Since Vietnam, interest rates offered to bigger savers with $100,000 to deposit rose sharply and then partially fell back several times, while small savers still received only 5¼ percent. The astute soon discovered access to Treasury bills, "locking in" far higher, government-backed interest rates, much higher than ordinary savings accounts provided.

As savings deposits were withdrawn, first in a trickle then a flow, to purchase these T-bills directly, the intermediary savings bankers began to speak of "disintermediation." However, Regulation Q prevented their paying any more to small savers, the working class, and retired elderly responsible for much of the savings.

Redlining (the practice in which banks refused ordinary home and improvement loan requests in older urban areas where many of their depositors lived) served to organize neighborhood interests who rightly feared that lack of conventional credit for sales and home improvements would cause deterioration. As government lending and insurance programs were introduced to fill the breach, many felt these were not just inferior, but actually spurred disinvestment. Communities sought congressional support in outlawing redlining. Hearings alone induced many banks to continue providing some long-term mortgages at fixed interest rates on the same terms as in the suburbs. Bankers, challenged by threats of antiredlining statutes and then by the Community Reinvestment Act, began to demonstrate renewed lending commitment to credit-worthy home buyers in stronger, urban neighborhoods—an initiative quickly dubbed "greenlining" and "gentrification" by their critics.

The little-noticed "secondary market" concept had been initiated back in 1938 through the Federal National Mortgage Association. FNMA was created as a mortgage dealer to provide banks additional money for lending by buying up old mortages and selling them to investors. Then in the mid-1960s, Congress created the Department of Housing and Urban Development (HUD) to achieve urban renewal, and merged into HUD the Federal Housing Administration (FHA), launched in 1934. Congress then instructed the FHA to insure urban mortgages involving lower-income home buyers and FNMA to buy these urban mortgages. Even as these initiatives were slowly being implemented, the rates of housing deterioration, abandonment, and acrimony rose. By the late 1970s, urban housing credit had become a very complex, bitter stew, involving too many interests to even be fully aware of one another.

Lenders, challenged by community interests, continued to make conventional fixed-interest, long-term mortgages to home buyers they judged credit worthy. Thus many urban bank lending portfolios now include mortgages to young, two-career households. At the time, 8 percent interest seemed high to the young buyers, and urban neighborhoods also seemed risky to the lenders. Today, however, these loans are sound but "under water," providing the lender with less return than must be paid to depositors to keep them from withdrawing the money covering those 8 percent mortgages. The "gentry" households now holding these mortgages would not dream of giving them up, "locking" many into owning. Not a few also bought adjoining properties as investments, tying up more mortgage credit.

Tax-exempt housing bonds began to attract attention as conventional interest rates rose with inflation. When conventional mortgage interest rates were 9 percent, tax-exempt bonds sold for around 6 percent. Investors in high tax brackets were willing to buy such tax-exempt state housing bonds. As interest rates climbed, many states created state housing finance agencies to be able to provide lower interest rates, but tax exemption required meeting some public purpose like housing rehabilitation or renewal of urban areas. Piggybacking credit from the sale of tax-exempt bonds on top of other government assistance programs became common practice in many states because this made the public purpose self-evident, but it resulted in extremely complex programs. Many tried valiantly to devise some way to link the ordinary home buyer with the lower interest rates provided by tax-exempt bonds, unaware that this involved many middlemen, underwriters, and brokerage houses, and really only matched the interest rates common a year or two earlier.

Many other potentially ominous side effects of this federal credit system also escaped common notice: the indirect tie-in to inflation, the growth of money market funds to enable smaller savers also to earn higher interest, the precarious financial position of many savings banks, and the growing influence of the secondary market and its housing-underwriting criteria on investment patterns.

A brief contrast here with other countries is illuminating. Canada's lenders are much fewer, larger, and more sophisticated. In the mid-1970s, they paid their savers more and stopped issuing fixed interest rate mortgages. The Canadian government also does not provide home owners with special tax deductions that increase with the taxpayer's tax bracket. In England, home buyers accepted renegotiable-rate mortgages (RRMs) years ago, recognizing that with inflation, their housing payments on outstanding loans would increase. Germany and France encourage savings specifically for home buying and target these efforts carefully. For example, Germany's *Bausparkassen*, savings-for-building institutions, will make a savings-mortgage contract with any would-be home owner. If a household regularly deposits savings into a special account providing below-market interest, then, once it reaches a preagreed personal savings target, it can obtain a below-market interest rate mortgage. The government also subsidizes this mortgage, but basically the *Bausparkassen* device simply links today's savers with tomorrow's borrowers in a separate market, an approach the U.S. government and home lenders ought to consider seriously.

The credit system in the United States, unlike any of those countries, has in effect separated saving from borrowing by offering high-interest money market funds on the one hand and fixed, low-interest, long-term mortgages on the other. For too long throughout the 1970s, federal Regulation Q limited small savers to below-market rates: 5¼ percent interest. This made the home owners' "windfall appreciation mortgage" possible, but now the savers' feeling of "being had," being paid so little and then taxed on this interest, has crippled the growth of conventional bank savings.

Home lending and savings in the United States now involve both a primitive cottage industry of 4,500 small lenders and some technologically very complex money market and secondary market institutions, which still have much to learn about housing, even as their procedures are already becoming difficult to alter. Sudden changes in housing investment patterns are now buffeting this Rube Goldberg system. Sophisticated home owners today retain their 8 percent mortgages much longer than before, while keeping their assets in money market funds at higher interest rates upon which they can draw checks. In the meantime the savings bankers have designed tax-exempt Individual Retirement Accounts (IRAs), and now mimic money market funds, hoping to capture new sources of money.

A Proliferation of New Mortgage Instruments

Lenders are backing away from holding long-term financial commitments themselves, selling them instead on the rapidly proliferating "secondary market," detailed in appendix B. At the same time, they are also developing a bewildering array of new mortgage instruments that relate to inflation in various ways, detailed in appendix C. Variable rate mortgages (VRMs) are linked to some index of the cost of money. Renegotiable rate mortgages (RRMs) allow the lender to renegotiate interest rates and payments during the term of the loan.

Graduated payment mortgages (GPMs) and shared appreciation mortgages (SAMs) are shakier concepts, counting on inflation and homeowner incomes to rise together. GPMs preschedule a rising series of monthly payments that do not even fully cover interest charges on the loan in the early years. This results in some negative amortization, owing more than initially borrowed for several years.

SAMs also count on housing inflation to continue, offering the home buyer a below-market interest rate mortgage in exchange for a share of the home's appreciation. Obviously, counting on inflation to continue, as well as household incomes to keep pace, constitutes a new kind of exposure for lenders, albeit different from the old exposure that initially got them into trouble: assuming that inflation would always be limited and the volume of passbook savings would steadily grow.

Ultimately the consumer and the secondary market will determine the future shape of mortgages. As long as consumers balk at high interest rates, indexing mortgage terms, or sharing their appreciation, such loans will not be issued. Since most banks also intend to resell them packaged into mortgage-backed securities, the secondary-market grading criteria will also influence their shape. Over time, however, some indexed version of variable or renegotiable rate mortgages seems likely to emerge as the conventional mortgage of the future.

Meanwhile, "creative financing" has become the newest thing enabling sales to continue in inflated market areas. Those already owning their homes for some time have a great deal of equity, the difference between its market value and what they still owe on the mortgage. Many minds have sought ways to take further advantage of this. Where a lower-interest, fixed-rate mortgage is still outstanding, many an owner has recently decided to retain it as long as possible. At the same time, lenders have tried to induce owners to pay their mortgages off before maturity or to renegotiate them. Some owners who must move on now simply rent rather than sell their homes. Others try to pass on the favorable financing along with the title, causing lenders to try to enforce the "due upon sale" clause often attached to it. Both home-owners' and lenders' rights are murkier than a reader of fine-print mortgage legalese might think. Courts in some states have not allowed banks to force an owner-seller to discharge an old mortgage; as long as this original owner continues making payments, he retains his advantageous financing, and then provides "seller financing."

The "wrap around" mortgage is a compromise to help the buyer who wants to assume the previous owner's mortgage but needs more credit. In this case the original lender wraps a new, higher-interest mortgage around the old one, resulting in financing that costs the buyer less than an entirely new mortgage but yields the lender a better return.

Sales now by elderly persons who own property free and clear sometimes involve even more unusual financing. An elderly owner may simply wish to remain in a small portion of the home, "sharing" it progressively over time with a new household, the buyer. They agree on a price, exchange a down payment, sign a balloon note for the balance in the future, and pay something "on account" in the interim. This mutually advantageous living arrangement resembles an accessory apartment in many ways. In situations where an owner has died and market prices are sky-high, yet financing costs seem even higher, even the heirs may act as lenders, receiving payments over time directly from the buyer, but often providing much more favorable terms than a conventional lender.

"Buy downs" are another new twist in selling property when the market fails because prices or financing costs are judged excessive. Here the nominal price remains, but in one way or another the buyer ends up with monthly payments at less than the full market rate of interest. As in a rebate, the seller or his broker may arrange "face-saving" financing.

"Reverse equity annuities" were another creative idea that passed from vogue before most people had even heard of the concept. The basic idea was a "reverse mortgage," enabling an elderly home owner to live off the equity in a home, receiving regular payments from a lender while more and more became owed to this lender. The problem was that, at high interest rates, a long-lived owner could soon end up owing the lender more than the house was worth, yet still not be ready to move out, while the heirs felt cheated out of their property.

All this razzle-dazzle in the credit world only obscures the disappearance of favorable fixed-rate, long-term financing for home ownership, the widely accepted "windfall mortgage." This was one of the two factors that made the middle-class home such a good investment during the 1970s. The other factor, home-owner income tax deductions, is the issue we consider next. Federal tax policies have by default become the dominant strand of national housing policy.

FEDERAL POLICIES AFFECTING HOUSING

Federal policies are currently shaping housing patterns in many complex and little understood ways. There are admittedly a myriad of federal actions, from mass transit aid to interstate freeways, from crime prevention to school busing and revenue sharing, that indirectly influence housing patterns, but these are outside our scope. The focus here is on direct housing assistance and several provisions of the tax code.

Direct Housing Assistance Raised Unattainable Expectations

Since the 1949 Housing Act, Congress has repeatedly reaffirmed the promise of "a decent home in a suitable living environment" for all

Americans. In recent years HUD regulations have emphasized that the home should also be affordable, stressing that housing costs should not exceed 25 percent of income. Only recently, under President Reagan, has 30 percent of income become the new yardstick.

Congress authorized $11.8 billion for housing programs in the 1981 budget, but only $5.5 billion are actually housing payments for all the subsidized rental units under HUD assistance programs, including Section 8. The balance goes toward community development block grants and demonstration projects. Drawn down at $3,000 or more per unit annually, the $5.5 billion in housing assistance can be aiding, at most, 2 million renter households. (The 1978 *Annual Housing Survey* indicated only 714,000 rental units with government rent subsidy as part of the stock, so the average drawdown costs were either higher or there were then a lot of commitments still outstanding for rehabilitation and new construction). In any case, adding these to the 1,934,000 units in public housing projects indicates that no more than 4 million renter households could be receiving direct government assistance. Yet most of the 14.4 million renter households with incomes under $10,000 must be spending over 25 percent of income on rent, if one interprets the 1978 *AHS* data and assumes ideal housing matches (see figure 2.1). If higher-income people are occupying some of the lower-cost private rentals, then the mismatch is even greater. Government rental assistance can be serving no more than a fraction of all the needy households, certainly less than one out of four. (Lowry estimates only 2.5 million out of 12.5 million low-income renters were helped, or one out of five.[3])

Heating a thermostat to make a room seem warmer is seen as a joke because we realize that the furnace is fooled and the room actually would become colder. Government rental assistance as recently administered by the Department of Housing and Urban Development is not unlike heating the thermostat, because it tends to supplant private housing production and maintenance and eliminates market controls of operating costs. As yet, few grasp how the much-publicized housing assistance interacts with the basic housing system. Most people have assumed that housing problems were being addressed, when in fact only a fraction could ever be served by the costly past programs like Section 8. Worse, indirect effects of federal tax policies were removing more rental stock and driving up prices for what remained, as elaborated in Chapter 3.

Many Americans, when asked about government housing assistance, think only of public housing and subsidized developments and ignore indirect tax expenditures. If they do consider the latter, they immediately think of obscure tax dodges they consider shady, such as double declining balance depreciation and tax syndication.

The reality is entirely different. In 1981, everyone's home-owner deductions added up to $31.8 billion, nearly three times the congressionally authorized housing programs, while investor deductions for rental housing amounted to $1.6 billion, only one-twentieth as much as the home-owner deductions.

Congressionally voted outlays, of course, are subject to far more budgetary scrutiny and debate than tax expenditures. A double standard divides indirect tax expenditures from the directly budgeted programs. The tax deductions are handled automatically by each eligible household on an annual basis, while housing assistance is fought over publicly, and twenty- to forty-year runout costs are mentioned by opponents to stress the heavy subsidies involved, as if they were direct handouts to the poor. Actually, most of the money goes to union-pay-scale labor and white-collar professionals who collaborate to produce and manage the housing. If the actual benefit of the budgeted housing programs is traced, it will be seen that the lion's share goes to more-advantaged persons.

The direct outlays committed to the housing programs in the federal budget have grown so little, they have barely kept pace with inflation in construction costs. Tax expenditures, however, automatically rise with mortgage interest rates and property taxes, compounded by the relief that tax shelters provide. As a result, tax expenditures are now *increasing annually* by more than the sum of all the budgeted programs.

The effects of the federal income tax code on housing are becoming increasingly important. For households in higher tax brackets, the tax code basically encourages living on credit by allowing interest expenses as tax deductions. It penalizes savers by taxing interest much like ordinary income. Resident home-ownership is further encouraged by allowing owners to deduct local property taxes from their taxable income, as well as by ignoring the value of the housing services provided by their homes. If the same dwelling were rented out, federal taxes would be due on the rental income. Even capital gains to resident owners are specially sheltered: they can be deferred if another home is bought within eighteen months, and owners aged fifty-five and over have a one-time $125,000 exemption.

While more elaborate tax provisions apply to rental real estate, their financial impact is much more limited. A percentage of the value of the structure, excluding the land, can be subtracted as depreciation from property income each year. If the expenses including depreciation more than offset the property income, the negative balance can shelter other income from taxes, or be syndicated to investors who seek such tax shelter. This depreciation ultimately becomes taxable upon sale of the property, but only at capital gains tax rates, which are much lower than the rates on ordinary income.

The economic impact of this tangle of federal tax provisions is best conveyed graphically. Figure 2.2, based on the statistics in table 2.2, is divided in two parts, illustrating both the housing elements in the federal

TABLE 2.2
Federal Housing Programs and Tax Expenditures

Housing Programs in the Federal Budget
(dollars in billions)

	1979	1980	1981
Community development block grants (CDBG)	$ 3.2	$ 3.5	$ 3.8
Urban development action grants (UDAGs)	—	.2	.4
Housing payments for all subsidized units under all HUD assisted programs	3.6	4.4	5.5
Other (Section 312, Self-help, etc.)	2.4	3.5	2.1
TOTAL OUTLAYS (NET) (Direct housing expenditures)	9.2	11.6	11.8

Housing Related Tax Expenditures, Fiscal Years 1977–1986
(dollars in billions)

	1977	1978	1979	1980	1981	1982	1983	1984	1985	1986
Home Owner Deductions										
Mortgage interest on owner-occupied homes	$ 4.5	$ 7.6	$ 10.7	$ 12.5	$19.8	25.3	31.1	37.9	46.3	56.5
Property tax on owner-occupied homes	4.2	5.5	6.8	7.7	8.9	10.7	12.7	15.2	18.0	21.5
Deferral and exclusion of capital gains on home sales	.9	1.1	1.4	1.5	1.7	1.9	2.1	2.3	2.5	2.7
Exclusion of interest on state and local housing bonds for owner-occupied housing	—	—	.1	.4	.8	1.2	1.6	1.9	1.8	1.8
SUB-TOTAL	9.6	14.2	19.0	22.1	31.3	39.1	47.5	57.2	68.7	82.5

Investor Deductions

Expensing of construction period interest and taxes	.2	.6	.6	.7	.8	.9	.9	1.0	1.1	1.1
Accelerated depreciation of rental housing	.3	.4	.4	.4	.4	.4	.5	.5	.5	.6
Exclusion of interest on state and local housing bonds for rental housing	—	.3	.4	.4	.6	.7	.8	.9	1.1
SUB-TOTAL	.5	1.3	1.4	1.5	1.6	1.9	2.1	2.3	2.5	2.8
TOTAL (housing related tax expenditures)	10.1	15.5	20.4	23.6	32.9	41.0	49.6	59.5	71.2	85.3
All federal tax expenditures		**133.9**	**158.0**	**176.9**						
Housing as a percent of total		11.6%	12.9%	13.3%						

NOTE: Tax expenditures are defined in the budget as "losses of tax revenue attributable to provisions of the federal income tax laws that allow a special exclusion, exemption, or deduction from gross income or provide a special credit, preferential rate of tax, or a deferral of tax liability affecting individual or corporate income tax liabilities."

SOURCE: Prepared by R. Goetze based on data compiled by Low Income Housing Information Service from *Special Analyses, Budget of the United States Government*, 1980, 1981; Projections by Joint Committee on Taxation and Congressional Budget Office (1981)

FIGURE 2.2
Federal Housing Programs and Tax Expenditures

HOUSING RELATED TAX EXPENDITURES
(dollars in billions)

Year	Value
1977	15.5
1978	20.4
1979	23.6
1980	32.9
1981	41.0
1982	49.6
1983	59.5

HOME-OWNER DEDUCTIONS
- property tax deductions
- mortgage interest deductions
- all other h.o. deductions

INVESTOR DEDUCTIONS

PROGRAMS IN BUDGET (VOTED BY CONGRESS):
- UDAGs
- other: 312 Self-help, etc.
- all payments for subsidized units under HUD
- CDBG

Year	Value
1979	9.2
1980	11.6
1981	11.8

SOURCE: Prepared by R. Goetze from data in Table 2.2

NOTE: CDBG = community development block grant
UDAG = urban development action grant

budget (below) and the tax deductions (above) in the same figure. The various deductions are called tax expenditures by analysts to suggest that they are "back door" costs—tax loopholes that could be altered or closed to produce more revenue and reshape the economy.

It has already been pointed out that the $31.3 billion in 1981 tax expenditures due to home-owner deductions are twenty times larger than the $1.6 billion of investor deductions. Taken together, the $32.9 billion in aggregate housing tax expenditures also dwarf the $11.8 billion budgeted by Congress for direct housing programs in 1981. The Congressional Budget Office estimates that, with rising mortgage interest rates and property taxes compounded by the higher tax brackets into which inflation has raised taxpayers, housing tax expenditures will soon be soaring by an additional $10 billion annually if the federal tax code is not changed, reaching $57.2 billion in fiscal 1984 and $82.5 billion in 1986.[4]

In 1980, before they began to soar, housing deductions at $23.6 billion were already over 13 percent of all tax expenditures. (See table 2.2.) The sharp increases in home-owner deductions shown in figure 2.2 make it likely that Congress will act before deductions reach the levels projected by the Treasury or that something else will countervail. Already, housing turnover has slowed.

The Inflationary Impact of Home-owner Deductions

Home-owner deductions are often defended as a necessary federal housing subsidy to keep home ownership affordable when, in fact, they have inflated the price of existing housing. In effect, they enable much of the expense of home ownership to be met with income before taxes—in contrast to tenants, who must pay their rent with after-tax dollars. A taxpayer in the 25 percent marginal tax bracket who pays $400 monthly in rent could choose home ownership instead of renting. As a home owner, if he deducts annual mortgage interest and property taxes from his income before figuring his federal tax liability, $500 pretax are the same to him as $400 after taxes. Another way of looking at this tax benefit is to consider that, in effect, it reduces a 13 percent mortgage interest rate to roughly 10 percent. The higher the tax bracket, the more these federal tax breaks extend home-buying power. A young, two-career household making $49,000 with no dependents easily finds itself in an over 40 percent tax bracket. Since this makes a 13 percent mortgage seem like less than 8 percent to them, this couple is very sensitive to the advantages of owning over renting.

The deductions are thus very regressive in their impact. The effective mortgage interest rate drops as the household's tax bracket increases. The rate of housing appreciation also appears to be a function of higher income appeal, although this effect is less consistent. These tax effects together produce a paradox: the same dwelling not only costs high-income households less to own; ownership also rewards them through appreciation in place of leaving them exposed to future rent increases.

The clearest insight into the way housing values inflate is gained through monitoring actual condominium conversions. Typically, apartments renting for $250 a month are worth at best four to six times the annual gross rent as apartment investments—that is, $12,000 to $18,000 per unit— because this market is depressed. However, marketed as condominiums, the same units start at ten times the annual gross rent, or $30,000, and maintain their value in the face of inflation. Rent controls, where present, may exaggerate the disparity. Most of the difference in value is not due to internal physical improvements, but to home-owner tax deductions and expectations of appreciation.

To buy the condominium requires a down payment and meeting substantial monthly costs for the mortgage and property taxes. For the household in a tax bracket above 40 percent, the interest on the money used for the down payment would be heavily taxed; instead the owner can deduct mortgage and property tax payments from his pretax income. The down payment also allows him to leverage his appreciation, which is further tax sheltered, although this is realized only upon sale. Thus it is easy to see how the market favors conversion, turning $12,000 – $18,000 rental headaches into appreciating $30,000 condominiums that also radically improve the local property tax base. The municipality and new buyers all benefit from this urban alchemy; but those displaced out by the process may not allow it to proceed.

Such appreciation has also been inflating existing single-family property values as home-owner deductions compound the effects of the windfall fixed-rate mortgage. These ownership incentives are unproductive wherever they spur speculating in existing housing rather than upgrading it and producing more, because they cause conversion of rental housing and divert funds from investing in industry. Because resident-owned housing is so tax sheltered, these tax and credit effects also increase the federal deficit.

Who Claims Home-owner Deductions?

Only one out of four taxpayers claims home-owner deductions, the younger and more affluent. We noted earlier that more than 90 percent of the home owners under forty-five had mortgages, while four out of five aged sixty-five and over did not. The tax savings are most attractive to younger households with higher incomes and substantial mortgage interest payments, the recent home buyers.

Figure 2.3 shows graphically home owners with tax deductions by income class in relation to all taxpayers, using 1979 data from the United

States Treasury Department, reproduced in table 2.3. It reveals that in 1979 $17.2 billion in mortgage interest and real estate tax savings were claimed on 23.7 million of the total 92.9 million tax returns. The three out of four taxpayers who did not claim these deductions were generally those with incomes under $20,000. The one out of four who did was at the high end. The shaded portions in figure 2.3 show the deductions claimed by the income groups between $15,000 and $30,000, the so-called middle class. The regressive nature of the deductions is evident upon inspection. The top bar (I) reveals that five-eighths ($10.7 billion in table 2.3) of the total homeowner tax expenditures were claimed by taxpayers over $30,000, those in the top one-ninth of the population, bar graph (B).

The percentage of taxpayers claiming these deductions increases sharply with income. The third bar graph (F) shows that most of those making under $15,000 did not claim these deductions. For 60 percent of the taxpayers, claiming such deductions was either not worth the bother or they were ineligible.

Table 2.3 provides more detail. In 1979 $4,369 billion in tax savings (25.4 percent of the total) were claimed by 8,153,000 taxpayers, one out of every two earning between $20,000 and $30,000. In this group those claiming deductions each had tax savings averaging $536.

In contrast, $1,245 billion in tax savings (7.2 percent of the total) were claimed by only 375,000 taxpayers at the top, 0.4 percent of all taxpayers. These households, six out of every seven earning over $100,000, each had tax savings averaging $3,320.

By 1981 the number of taxpayers earning over $100,000 had almost doubled to 775,000.[5] Of these, 670,000 took property tax deductions averaging $1,927, and 406,000 took mortgage interest deductions saving each an average of $3,626. The average tax saving for those claiming both had risen to $5,553. The shift of all taxpayers into higher tax-paying brackets by inflation, a phenomenon dubbed "tax bracket creep" by the media, lies behind the Congressional Budget Office (CBO) estimates of accelerating homeowner deductions in coming years. The passage of the 1981 Tax Act moderates these projections, but the basic trend still holds.

Other Secondary Effects of Home-owner Deductions

While some may have realized that tax favoritism for housing disproportionately benefits the well-to-do, it is not widely recognized how these tax benefits contribute to general inflation. In addition to directly bidding up housing prices, this system is also raising the cost of borrowing. Paradoxically, these rising prices have made more people strive to become home owners. A generation ago it made economic sense to save up for a down payment on a home, borrow as little as possible, and to pay off the

TABLE 2.3
Revenue Costs of Home-owner Deductions by Income Class

(1979 Law, 1979 Levels)

Expanded Income Class ($000)	Number of Total Returns (1000s)	(%)	Returns with Tax Deductions Number of Returns (1000s)	(%)	Percent of all Returns Filed in Class (%)		Average Tax Savings Returns with Deductions (dollars)	Total Revenue Cost ($ millions)		Revenue Cost as Percent of Total Tax Paid by Members of Class (%)
(A)	(B)	(C)	(D)	(E)	(F)	(G)	(H)	(I)	(J)	(K)
Under 5	21,630	23.3%	83	0.3%	0.42	$ 5K	$ 104	$ 9	—	
5–10	18,670	20.1	1,083	4.6	5.8	10k	172	187	1.1%	2.6%
10–15	14,510	15.6	2,553	10.7	17.6	15K	254	649	3.8	3.7

15–20	22,880	12.8	3,955	16.6	33.3		331	1310	7.6	5.4
20–30	15,700	17.0	8,153	34.3	51.7	20K	536	4,369	25.4	8.3
30–50	8,020	8.6	5,924	24.9	73.9	30K	1,023	6,058	35.1	11.9
50–100	2,000	2.1	1,658	7.0	82.9	50K	2,048	3,395	19.7	11.0
100 & Over	400	0.5	375	1.6	85.6	100K	3,320	1,245	7.2	4.1
TOTAL	92,920	100.0	23,785	100.0	25.6		$ 724	$17,221	100.0	8.1%

SOURCE: Prepared by R. Goetze from Treasury Department data that appear in the U.S. Department of HUD, *1980 Housing Production Report*, appendix A.

NOTES: Columns I, B, and F were used to generate figure 2.3.
Details may not add to totals because of rounding.
$5K = $5000

Reprinted with permission of the Lincoln Institute of Land Policy.

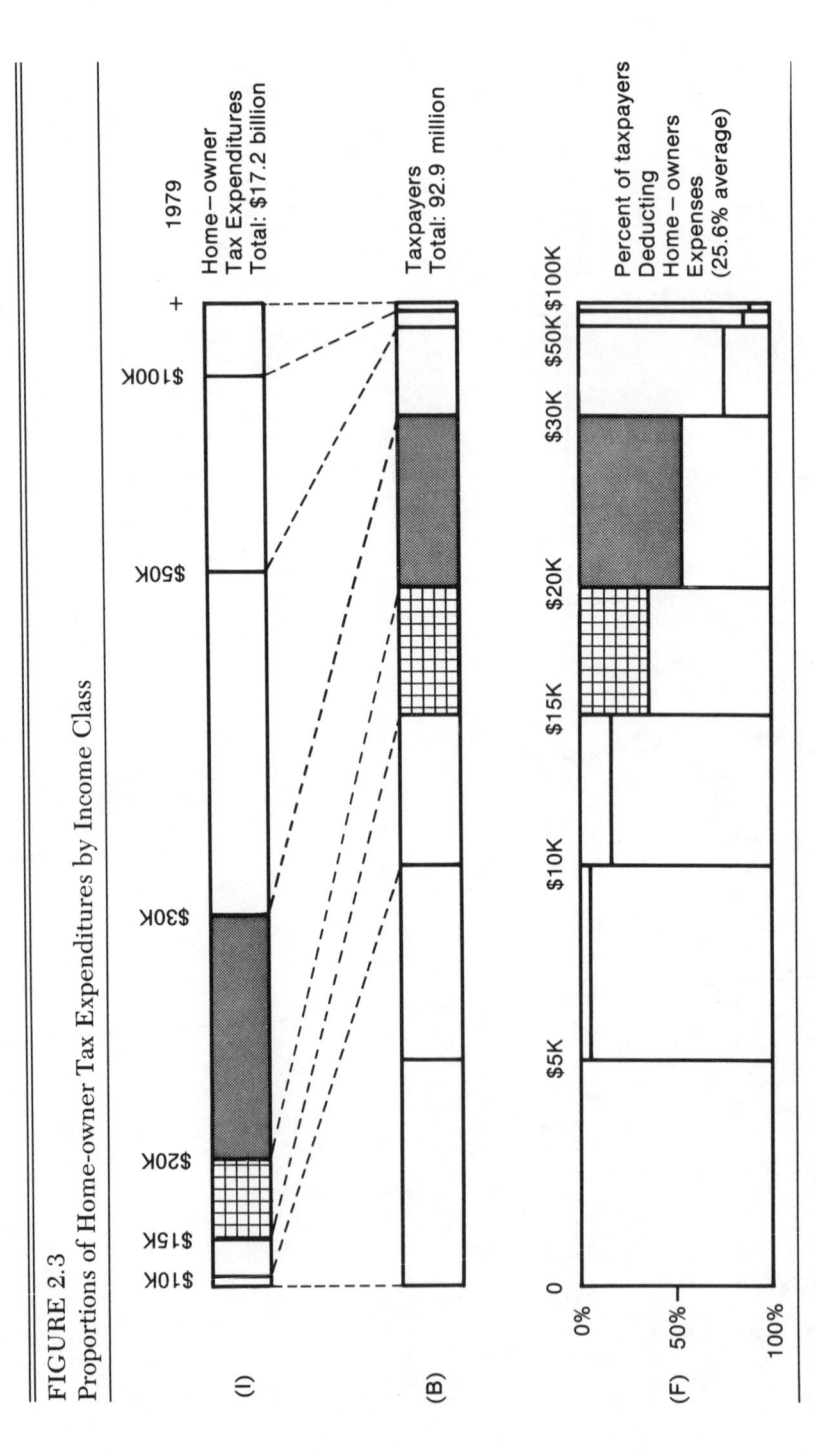

FIGURE 2.3
Proportions of Home-owner Tax Expenditures by Income Class

SOURCE: U.S. Treasury Department; see table 2.3.
NOTE: $5K = $5,000

mortgage. The pot of gold was yours after paying off the mortgage; the ethic involved getting free of debt.

During the 1970s, achieving housing appreciation with borrowed, fixed-interest money looked better and better. Savings produced negative interest, while borrowing produced tax deductions. The down payment was scrounged from the parents, no longer saved. The class consequences of this shift are profound: home ownership, which a generation ago was widely available to the working poor, became a form of patrimony, available mainly to the children of the affluent.

With fewer people saving less and more people borrowing more, the cost of mortgage money was simply bid up, automatically producing still bigger tax deductions, bigger federal deficits, and inflating the housing component of the consumer price index. This in turn triggered higher social security checks, bigger wage demands on the part of government workers and industry, and largely futile demands for direct housing subsidies to the poor, further unbalancing the federal budget.

In part, the interaction between tax policies and housing inflation has been misunderstood because it is so full of paradoxes. In theory, tax subsidies to a particular sector ought to induce greater supply in response to the after-tax attractiveness of the investment. In the long run this still holds true, but the theory breaks down in the face of shortages because housing takes so long to build and lasts so long. Tax benefits stimulate more demand, but producers cannot produce enough new housing where people now seek it. The result is higher prices for what there is, while new production falters.

James M. Poterba, of the National Bureau of Economic Research, has modeled the housing system and concludes that these tax-inflation interactions could be responsible for as much as a 30 percent increase in housing prices.[6] Another economist, Patric H. Hendershott, has developed an abstract econometric macrohousing model from which he concludes that higher housing costs nonetheless favor home ownership over rental.[7] He estimates that, without this bias, 4½ to 5 million fewer of the nation's 77 million households would have been home owners at the end of 1978.

While one can quibble with such models and their particular assumptions, the general pattern is becoming quite noticeable if one looks for it in cities. Examining neighborhoods in a whole range of cities across the nation makes it clear that such housing appreciation does not occur evenly across the board. In areas of perceived housing shortages, prices are inflated sharply because housing is increasingly bought as a hedge against inflation. Here, the nest has become the nest egg, to be protected at all costs. As more people hear of appreciation in an area, more want to climb aboard there. Meanwhile, disinvestment continues in nearby neighborhoods. This urban rediscovery only began with Victorian "treasure" but now feeds on adjoining stock, including rental apartments, converting them to condominiums.

Policy makers need to take note of this trend now because its urban impact is only just beginning. Until the 1970s, these deductions were mainly claimed on new suburban, single-family housing. With the emergence of a new back-to-the-city focus in settlement patterns, these tax expenditures could provide the driving force to recycle much of the urban rental stock that is in economic distress.

Urban revitalization and conversion of rental stock to condominiums seemed initially in everyone's best interest because it was thought only luxury rentals would be converted. In Boston, for example, aggregate statistics still suggest that luxury conversions dominate in the 2 percent of the stock that has been converted, but closer inspection reveals that the condominium conversion process only begins with the better stock in any specific market area. Once the up-market becomes established, it can quickly spread to affect other stock in the same area like lodging houses previously housing poorer people, and even nonresidential structures.

From the urban policy perspective, such effects of the federal tax code on existing housing were quite unanticipated. In the past, under filtration, these home-owner deductions served to offset some of the costs of buying new suburban housing. Turnover in due course to others down the line in suburbia was taken for granted. Home-owner deductions may not have been intended to produce new housing, but for generations they served well for this purpose. Now, however, many unexpected forces are coming together to change the housing picture.

HOW HOUSING FUNDAMENTALS HAVE RECENTLY CHANGED

Private housing development has become more and more difficult as antigrowth attitudes spread. Developers are often confronted by zoning constraints, complex permit requirements, and labor regulations. Astronomical financing costs make any delays disastrous. As a result, new housing in desirable locations has become so costly that attractive, already-existing stock has often soared in value. This is a departure from the widely accepted "hand-me-down" or "filtration" theory. The traditional appeal of a new home in a suburban subdivision has also diminished as new life-styles generate new demand patterns. Since building new in closer-in, built-up areas costs even more, adaptive reuse of existing structures is further enhanced. Beyond already being in the right "location," these often provide low acquisition costs, appealing and high-quality original workmanship plus extras such as hardwood, period detailing, stained glass transoms, or more generous storage areas.

There is now widespread policy debate about rising housing costs and unaffordability. Resident ownership has developed a distinct edge in holding down operating costs, while the traditional advantage of low acquisition costs in rental housing has eroded. Inflation has exacerbated the disparities.

To buy a home or renew a lease obviously costs more after years of inflation and higher interest rates, but what rate of increase is fair? The congressionally endorsed guideline, 25 percent of income (recently raised to 30 percent), only adds to the confusion. Those who exceeded 35 percent of income to acquire a home in 1970 discovered a few years into home ownership that they were spending well under 25 percent and leveraging appreciation. Today, however, more and more people consider it impossible to embark on home ownership.

AHS statistics were used to show that there already was a deficit of many millions of affordable rental units under $146 per month in 1978. Surely this situation has since worsened. In many areas, rents then did not meet costs. In weak market areas with poor, elderly tenants, most landlords sought few rent increases and skimped on maintenance. But as more affluent, young professionals appeared, rents often rose sharply. Interventions, intended to keep rents affordable, inadvertently drove up operating costs and encouraged sales, thereby increasing debt service. The result is a further reduction in value of rental investments, favoring the best properties for conversion to condominiums.

Differentiating operating from acquisition costs, as well as separating rental housing economics from resident ownership, helps us understand the current situation. This is basic to considering what could now be done to hold down housing costs.

Operating costs tend to be efficiently controlled under home ownership because the investor and the resident are one and the same. Decisions regarding levels of heat, utilities, maintenance, management, and periodic upgrading are internalized or easily reached.

In the rental situation, however, the interests of the investor, manager, lender, residents, and repairmen are separated out, allowing conflicts to arise. In the past, under tenancy-at-will and before much inflation, rising operating costs were sometimes discussed with tenants, sometimes simply stated by the landlord, and generally passed along where possible. With multiyear leases, rent adjustments became more erratic. Many owners experiencing rising heating expenses, higher repair costs, and more property taxes were held back from passing them along to current residents, waiting instead until turnover or lease renewal. This made matching cost increases to inflation a disjointed process breeding mistrust and confrontations. Tenants became aware of sizable rent increases upon turnover or lease renewal without considering all the years that rents were held back.

Acquisition costs are usually financed, which adds debt service to monthly operating costs. For home buyers, acquisition costs always loomed large compared to operating costs, since for them a much larger share of monthly housing costs goes toward paying off the amortizing mortgage. As already described, this housing expense is tax sheltered, and provides the owner equity and appreciation.

In the rental situation, lenders were often content with nonamortizing mortgages until the 1960s, in effect "renting" investor owners the use of capital in return for a fixed rate of interest, and rolling over the balloon mortgage every five years or so. This meant that *operating costs* were the dominant factor as rental owners sought a steady return on investment.

As blight and deterioration became urban issues, lenders began calling for amortization, mortgages paying off principal. This sharply raised debt service.

Government interventions designed to improve rental cash flow were ultimately counterproductive because of their indirect but inflationary effects on expenses. Public interventions at the federal level involved allowing accelerated depreciation and providing subsidies to qualified units; and on the local level, trying to regulate rents and conversions.

Accelerated depreciation allows investor owners to reduce their taxes by increasing their nominal expenses. The intent was to make marginal housing investments more attractive through tax concessions, but inadvertently this transformed investor ownership. These tax provisions drew in more sophisticated operators, seeking not a steady, fair return from rental operations, but hungry for capital appreciation through the buying, selling, and trading of properties. Because the tax benefits of accelerated depreciation rapidly taper off, these provisions encourage rolling over ownership prematurely. Such turnover in the face of rising mortgage interest rates requires even more rent dollars to service debt, leaving less money to meet operating costs and maintenance expenses in the long run.

Federal rental assistance payments under Section 8, like earlier mortgage subsidies, served to obscure actual rental housing costs. Municipalities frequently employed these subsidies (matching them with other resources like community development block grants) to restore the most deteriorated housing that could still be salvaged. In market contexts where such stock had no buyers and the market value of the best was no more than $10,000 per unit, the assistance allowed up to $50,000 per unit to be spent on acquisition and substantial rehabilitation. These subsidies were extremely popular because they improved the targeted housing as well as profited all those directly involved, at the same time that they reduced the rent burden upon tenants. With limited funds, however, many cities qualified only those properties sufficiently deteriorated. By rewarding only the worst housing and that so favorably, the assistance discouraged proper maintenance of all the other marginal stock, as its owners allowed deterioration to continue to the point where they, too, might qualify for Section 8 aid. There developed a real dependence upon ever more federal assistance, which the federal government appears no longer willing to sustain.

Local rent control ordinances are often passed to prevent sharp rent *increases*, but once enacted they mobilize a political constituency aimed at *freezing* rents. This discourages not only proper maintenance but any further new development without subsidies. As only limited subsidized production continues, housing shortages become more acute, stepping up demand for the remaining stock.

All of these public interventions to reduce the rent burden on assisted tenants aimed at symptoms. They all had short-sightedness in common. None reached the root of rising costs: increasing friction and polarization among the housing supplier and consumer interests. Rather, they only compounded the factors driving up costs: turnover, disinvestment, and poor coordination. Their promises of benefits to those involved are eventually dwarfed by less direct and longer-range effects still not fully apparent. The blame for these housing interventions is systemic. Blame should not be limited to the individuals who accelerate depreciation or rehabilitate with Section 8, nor on those who seek rent controls. Instead we must realize how all these provisions acting together contribute to the erosion of rental housing and needlessly drive up the costs of providing housing services from the stock that remains.

Incentives that *discourage* title turnover and help longer-term owners maintain and make modest improvements would have been much more beneficial because these incentives minimize increases in operating and debt service costs. Housing allowances (rent vouchers) can act as such incentives (described in chapter 4). Even a broader Section 8 existing program could have been revised to operate this way.

The rental housing system has come to involve more and more actors in increasingly conflicting roles. Many tenants cannot afford the rising rents resulting from needless turnover which raises both debt service and operating costs. Differences that tenant and landlord used to settle between themselves or were forced to live with now involve so many interests, policies, boards, and procedures that actions are disjointed, increasing mistrust and driving up costs. As interests that must work together become polarized, available resources are spent less effectively. In such situations, simple operating matters like fixing a leaky facet, bathroom drain, or gutter are often ignored until more serious damage has occurred.

Conversely, in resident ownership many operating responsibilities converge upon the home owner, encouraging him to address problems in a timely, efficient manner. For a home owner to get back at himself, the way some tenants try to get back at their landlord, would be absurd. Yet this reveals why operating costs, for similar housing services, are so much lower under home ownership.

Acquisition costs, however, have become a critical hurdle for new home buyers. Now, earlier buyers stay put because by retaining title they retain their favorable financing. However, they thereby become "locked in," keeping out the next wave of home seekers. These, unwilling to meet current prices, are instead devising innovative routes to home ownership that enable them to substitute ingenuity, sweat equity (do-it-yourself labor), and self-enterprise for some of the tens of thousands of dollars others now pay for homes in move-in condition.

Multifamily properties *as rentals* have become a relatively unattractive asset today because of rising operating costs. Promises of more federal subsidies and lower finance costs through tax-exempt state financing only masked this. The increased demand for home ownership is reaching over to that portion suitable for luxury rentals or conversion to condominiums. Tenant advocates argue that rents in existing housing have risen too much, but in fact operating costs, hassles, and debt service have risen even more. These have risen so much that multifamily properties are worth less and less owned as rentals. Converted to condominiums, however, they are worth more.

Moving, at current rents and prices, is no longer viable in many markets. Judging housing affordability on the basis of "25 percent of income" is thus a great oversimplification. Costs enter in upward lurches upon turnover. For new home owners, acquisition costs now require a much heavier initial sacrifice than only a few years ago, because existing homes became priced not as hand-me-downs but as inflation hedges for the affluent. Those buying from now on with indexed mortgages may not quickly find their housing costs so favorable, but in the long run they will at least be better off than tenants, because they can effectively control operating costs and gain at least equity if not some appreciation.

For tenants, however, still accustomed to 1970s' rents and viewing housing costs in relation to their current incomes, the future looks increasingly grim. World forces are driving everyone to greater self-reliance or doing without—and tenants cannot escape these macroforces. Just as renting a car is an expensive convenience compared to owning, renting a home is also becoming a luxury because operating costs are handled so inefficiently. Indeed, rentals were considered suited for those who could not afford ownership due to an anomaly. Like hand-me-downs and used cars in an era of surplus, used housing could be obtained for just its operating costs. Today, as scarcities loom and throwaways vanish, development and acquisition costs have reemerged as an integral part of housing costs that residents must either pay (even if it requires doubling up) or that institutions must pay on their behalf. Landlords and the federal government now seem less and less inclined to subsidize tenants.

Existing rental housing can only survive through more efficient uses of available resources. This includes retaining the lower interest financing many current owners still hold, and finding the proverbial stitch in time, instead of looking for new subsidies and tax gimmicks. Increasing tenant responsibilities and their awareness of the current situation could also moderate rent increases. Nevertheless, even if the counterproductive public interventions were rescinded, broader, shallower demand-side subsidies will still be needed to avert more erosion of rental housing.

IN CONCLUSION

New housing construction has become increasingly complex. Zoning regulations, multiple permit requirements, as well as other local conditions now convey an anti-growth attitude that discourages building even upper-income housing. While home-owner tax incentives are not strong enough to offset these development constraints, they encourage conversion and reuse of existing housing as life-styles and housing demands change. Out in most suburbs, a significant amount of empty-nester housing is coming on the market or spawning new accessory apartments to match whatever demand there is. In the urban areas to which excess demand has suddenly shifted, red tape confronting new construction is even more complex. The federal and state housing subsidies, which until recently assisted developers there overcome delays and neighborhood opposition, have been cut back.

Two-career life-styles and concerns about rising energy and commuting costs are altering traditional settlement patterns. For increasing numbers, the importance of a suburban home, yard, and schools has declined, along with the interest in raising a family—at least for the time being. Home-owner tax deductions remain as the principal housing subsidy, too weak to produce new development but fostering the discovery of overlooked urban housing opportunities instead. Since structures already exist, there are few permit hassles, and the prices seem favorable to the more affluent. Investor-owners, who have taken their accelerated depreciation and now seek to turn over their rental properties, are beginning to sell three- to six-unit structures to new young resident owners. Many are deciding that instead of spending $100,000 on a single family home out in the suburbs, they can buy a more convenient and unusual urban residence for less. This arrangement has a silver lining: tenants who contribute rental income to help pay the mortgage and also provide greater residential security while the owners are out. However, at current mortgage interest rates, rents higher than those of the past are inevitable, so these new buyers usually end up bringing in new households like themselves as tenants.

Throughout the unsubsidized rental housing stock, traditional rents are rising upon turnover, after long being sheltered from inflation. For some time, many owners deferred selling in the hopes that a drop in interest rates would revive rental property values, creating a backlog of properties ripe for turnover. Tax provisions increasingly encourage selling by those who took advantage of accelerated depreciation. Today, however, high mortgage interest rates make multiunit properties no longer affordable as rentals without federal assistance after turnover.

A wide range of new types of buyers has emerged to replace the traditional stable investor in rental property. These new buyers variously contemplate renting to much more affluent tenants, converting to condominiums, rehabilitating with Section 8 assistance, speculating or profiting from the disinvestment "end game," and even gaining from arson-for-profit.

Apartments, Homes, and Projects
IN MORE DETAIL 3

PRIVATE MULTIFAMILY RENTAL HOUSING IN JEOPARDY

One hears that much rental housing is in grave difficulty, yet some twenty-seven million American households, one in every three, still rent. In many older urban areas, two out of three households are tenants. The future of rental housing now seems shrouded in polarized debate. Tenants often consider talk of rent increases simply ludicrous. Many tenants already view conditions as mediocre at best and consider their current rents unaffordable. At the same time, many investor-owners have become convinced that their return on investment in rental housing has become so unattractive that they had better withdraw from the business. Money market certificates offer them a much better return with no headaches and little risk.

In the meantime, public attempts to regulate rents, conditions, evictions, and conversions please few. Conventional financing has been largely withdrawn and replaced by many new wrinkles; sellers are taking back mortgages here; newcomers are forming unconventional investment pools there. Buyers either seek state tax-exempt financing and count on a stream of long-term federal rental assistance or intend to convert to condominiums. However, because there is neither suitable credit nor sufficient assistance to finance turnover, many existing owners feel stuck, unable to extricate themselves from their unproductive holdings. How these dilemmas will actually be resolved is hard to predict.

In chapter 2 the notion was put forth that recently some rental housing was treated as a throwaway. Much hand-me-down housing was left behind after the middle class moved to FHA-insured suburban home ownership. With little maintenance, low interest mortgages, and pre-OPEC energy prices, a few dollars rented a lot of space. Rentals were not in the best locations, perhaps, but in hindsight, they appear to have been a bargain, since rents did not fully cover maintenance and replacement costs.

Even though national trends in rental housing have received much attention, few clear recommendations have emerged. A host of housing specialists including Anthony Downs, George Sternlieb, Ira Lowry, and Patric Hendershott were convened by HUD to summarize their conclusions at the Conference on the Rental Housing Crisis, November 14, 1980.

Lowry captured the basic debate by contrasting the U.S. General Accounting Office report, *Rental Housing: A National Problem that Needs Immediate Attention* (1979), with the Pollyana Institute's *Rental Housing: Two Decades of Progress*(1980).[1] He summarized that GAO report as follows:

> The GAO finds that renters' choices are being progressively restricted even as their real housing cost burdens increase; landlords are going broke; and private investors are shying away from an obviously unprofitable market. Although the federal government subsidizes a significant share of the market, the need for assistance far exceeds the government's present ability to provide it. Of 12.5 million low-income renters, only about 2.5 million were helped by federal programs.[2]

Quite different reading of the same data emerged in the "Pollyana Institute report" cited by Lowry:

> The past two decades have seen steady improvement in the housing circumstances of renters, especially those with low incomes. Rents in constant dollars have dropped, per capita housing consumption by renters has increased, and the incidence of both overcrowding and major housing defects has diminished sharply. Millions of single adults, formerly constrained to live with relatives, have been able to afford separate homes—either living alone or with friends. The supply of suburban rental dwellings has increased, widening the locational options of those who prefer renting to owning. And for renters who prefer owning, the opportunities have seldom been better.[3]

Is the glass half empty or half full? Lowry points out that the two studies used essentially the same data base, but that the GAO report treats the rental market demand as a fixed set of households whose rents and incomes were changing. The Pollyana Report suggests that household structure itself was changing in response to rising income and housing market conditions.

Population immediately diffused into any inventory enlargement. Sternlieb has a catchy summary for this interpretation of the demographics: "Inexpensive housing supply begets households." Assuming that renter households remained unchanged led to overly pessimistic views like the GAO's.

Indeed, the rise in housing consumption during the 1970s was unprecedented. The 14 percent increase in the number of renter households took place with only a 1 percent increase in the total population living in such households. Real income per capita fell by only 8 percent while real housing consumption per capita increased 22 percent. The number of rooms per person also rose by 13 percent, and other indices of housing quality also improved.[4] Common sense suggests that such "progress," measured against untethered expectations, could not continue forever.

To explain low vacancies and uneconomic rents, Lowry proposes the notion of "excess capacity," suggesting that owners avoid vacancies by renting out their stock at whatever rents the market provides. In areas that are overbuilt, or where renters' population has decreased, such rents are below long-run average cost. Low vacancy rates thus would indicate neither an impending shortage of rental units nor that returns were adequate to maintain the stock—two common misconceptions that have derailed rental housing policies.

From the many tenants' perspectives, such overviews may be statistically correct, but they ignore *perceptions*. Where people want to live and how they feel about housing costs there shape behavior. An average vacancy rate or rent means little if, compared to each mover household's *expectations,* the only homes available seem "crummy" or overpriced. Everyone knows the person who still expects to get a good steak dinner or a decent shirt for $4.95 is likely to be disappointed. In seeking a new rental, however, tenants do not shop regularly; instead, they have in mind what they used to pay or the government yardstick, 25 percent of household income. Moreover, their outrage about rent increases now occurring in the desirable neighborhoods (read: revitalizing or gentrifying) is newsworthy even before such new rents are statistically detectable.

Before discussing what could happen next, changes already occurring must first be understood. Former rental households were not static, but responded in various ways. Many, particularly husband-wife households, became home owners, often leaving members behind; others split up. Those remaining renters during the 1970s were the female-headed, black, or elderly households. Since home ownership provided better rewards to those in higher tax brackets, it should be no surprise that renters are now increasingly lower-income households, the residuals not rewarded by home-owner tax deductions.

If renters can afford only underutilized stock, then in strong market areas they will now have to begin to double up or look for "excess capacity" in new ways, like splitting up larger housing units. The most promising new housing surplus is in larger single-family homes owned by empty-nesters. In 1978, the *Annual Housing Survey* shows, there were 12.2 million one- or two-person home-owner households headed by someone aged fifty-five or older (including 7.3 million aged sixty-five and over) living in homes containing five rooms or more. Here accessory apartments could easily be created, an issue explored more fully in the next section, resident-owned homes.

Rents Are Increasingly Inadequate for Proper Maintenance

In the traditional multifamily rental stock, the 1980 U.S. census reveals that $200 to $250 is now a common monthly rent, but this is misleading, based on out-of-date financing and undermaintenance. To maintain the stock properly would cost considerably more, as much as $400 to $500 monthly for the typical unit after ownership turnover with private financing. Wherever economic rents cannot be obtained from residents or via subsidies, disinvestment will worsen. For years many owners held off making repairs, selling, or refinancing, expecting the values of rental properties to rise, but these actions cannot be postponed indefinitely. If the rental stock is to be maintained, improvements are long overdue. Over the next five years there will also inevitably be many sales and transfers, worsening the current predicament. Understanding this requires recapitulating some history.

A simple multiplier, typically five to eight times annual gross rents, was used to value rental properties in the 1960s, when rents under $100 monthly were common. Thus a ten-unit property renting for $100 per month would have been judged worth $60,00–100,000 ($100 × 12 × 10 × 5 = $60,000), depending primarily on its location and quality. Slightly more sophisticated investors would look at the net, the difference between rental income and operating expenses before financing. The capitalization rate, derived from the sales of similar properties, served to relate the annual net income from a particular property to its hypothetical value. For example, a "cap" rate of 9 percent (normal when mortgage interest was around 6 percent and risks were moderate) served to value a property netting $7,000 annually as worth about $78,000 ($7,000/.9 = $77,777). The higher the risk or the interest rate, the lower the value. At that time owning such rental properties seemed like owning a high-grade bond, providing a predictable return on investment. Owners then still considered positive cash flow as the primary return on their investment.

Such rules of thumb were used, not only by investors to spot "bargains" when offered for less, but also by lenders and insurers to determine mortgage limits and insurance coverage. However, rising mortgage interest rates and higher urban risks quickly raised the cap rate during the 1970s to 16 or even 20 percent. A property netting $12,000 after expenses thus was still worth only $75,000 ($12,000/.16 = $75,000). So, even when the net income kept pace with post-Vietnam inflation, the change in capital costs resulted in no appreciation or even declining values for most rental properties during the 1970s. The public still thought landlords were making out like bandits and often sought rent controls. However, where these effectively held down the owner's net, his income after expenses, they made poor investments worse.

Insurers, appraisers, and tax assessors, also unaware of basic market changes, frequently continued using the simpler rules of thumb—for example, value is "five times gross rent." This provided owners more insurance coverage or credit than properties were actually worth, and imposed unfair tax burdens. In particular instances where the owner then failed to meet all his responsibilities, taxes went unpaid. Sometimes the creditors or insurers also became exposed to risk. Charles Abrams, the housing guru, once told of a banker moving to foreclose on a declining New York property only to discover that its owner, with gallows humor, had already transferred its title to a Bowery bum. More recently, when insurance coverage exceeded market value, arson for profit became a way of "selling the building to the insurance company." Such basic shifts in the market are much easier to identify in hindsight than at the time they were occurring.

Well-intentioned policies to promote rehabilitation and cure blight in existing housing began in earnest in the War on Poverty, but indirectly they worsened long-run rental economics by obscuring not only income and expenses, but actual demand and supply as well. Nonprofit ownership, government-insured mortgages, below-market-rate federal financing, and allowing accelerated depreciation in calculating federal tax liabilities—all were intended to promote better rental housing, but they masked important elements of market value and risk. Many neophytes entered the real estate business after 1965 in response to these incentives, only to find themselves the owners of overpriced stock unloaded by shrewder investors.

Urban housing was out of fashion for a score of years while the nation, preoccupied with suburban child-rearing, overbuilt its housing stock. Because of slack urban demand, rents in general were below the break-even point. Much urban housing stock began to filter rapidly down toward abandonment.

Overbuilding was an underlying cause of urban abandonment, obscured by much finger-pointing among ineffective local officials, redlining banks, frustrated residents, grandstanding politicians, and unscrupulous real estate interests. Suburban overbuilding allowed many urban problems to surface, like racial steering and redlining by brokers, insurers, and lenders. Addressing these in isolation could not cure housing deterioration and abandonment.

If there had been less growth in supply during the 1970s, however, then housing standards could have been enforced. Proper maintenance would have cost only another $30–40 a month back then, and much more stock would have been maintained and thereby saved.

Federal policy instead provided an extra $200 and more monthly *per unit* to redevelopers of showcase projects in deteriorating areas, further siphoning off demand for conventional rentals and distorting resident expectations in these neighborhoods. Housing codes became unenforceable because most rental incomes were inadequate and tenants could always move on to the next hand-me-down.

The illustrative $200 monthly rent is, therefore, the product of outdated financing and a disinvestment psychology still shared by too many lenders, owners, and tenants. In today's dollars, $250 monthly would provide a break-even rent for stock still in adequate repair, and perhaps $350 would induce the necessary upgrading by existing owners to make up for deferred maintenance. Title turnover and refinancing adds another $100–$150 monthly to rents with no visible improvements. This only introduces current capital costs. The difference between 6 percent and 16 percent on a $12,000 mortgage is $100 a month, without any upgrading. It even limits the owner's return on equity to levels that seemed inadequate years ago.

Sales and refinancing were postponed for years in the hopes that finance costs would come back down, but current owners will not own and defer repairs forever. Financing now, at interest rates above 16 percent and hard to obtain, renders this stock worth little *as rental housing*. Table 3.1 shows these rent relationships for the "same" unit.

TABLE 3.1
Various Illustrative Rents for the "Same" Unit

	"Disinvestment" Deferred Maintenance	Break-even	"Gentrification" Upgrading
Under current ownership	$200/mo	$250/mo	$350/mo
After turnover*	300/mo	375/mo	500/mo

*If turnover not obtainable, disinvestment accelerates.
SOURCE: Prepared by R. Goetze from housing interviews in the Boston area.

Home-owner tax deductions compound the problem by limiting obtainable rents. Most households that can afford $500 monthly are already in a tax bracket that makes resident ownership much more advantageous. ($417 per month is one-quarter of a $20,000 annual income.)

If rents cannot be raised to these levels, then the owner's net income drops so low that the structure would be worth less than two years' gross rents at current capitalization rates. Under such a foreshortened time horizon, no rational owner would undertake any improvements; rather, he would simply allow the property to run down, and stop paying local taxes to salvage what he could.

Rental housing is caught in a fatal dilemma. Really improving rental housing and passing through the effects of inflation requires roughly a doubling of rents. However, the 12.5 million or more tenant households that currently feel hard pressed will find such rent increases intolerable.

In the meantime, some of the baby-boom households are taking a fresh look at urban living, providing an alternative market for this stock. Tenants are used to moving, but now someone has already bought "the next dwelling" as an investment, either to reside in or to convert to condominiums. This rental housing may no longer be profitably rented to moderate income tenants, but the same stock converted to condominiums is often attractive to more affluent homeowners.

Frequently Suggested "Solutions" to Aid Tenants Are Too Limited

Not every householder is suited to become a home owner. Particularly the elderly and those who must move frequently cannot shoulder the responsibilities of ownership. Even though the long-term trend toward home ownership continues, a residual tenant population will remain. A range of new housing solutions is being proposed to address their needs; these vary in cost, practicality, tenant appeal, and political acceptability. They may help some. But if they are viewed as general solutions, they are worse than doing nothing, because even together they cannot significantly improve the basic rental housing predicament. I mention them only briefly before discussing ways to buy more time for those who remain tenants.

Paying much more per square foot or doubling up will be the tenants' recourse if nothing is done. As yet, these do not seem to be politically acceptable options because they imply curtailed choices and a drop in the American standard of living. People still seem eager to grasp at more quick fixes.

Revitalization is often promoted by interests working through local governments without regard for the underlying economics. Municipal real estate tax incentives like New York's J-51 tax abatements encourage fix-up, but only the more affluent can afford the resulting housing. In fact, real estate interests, lenders, and local officials all share in the benefits of private revitalization, rising property values, and an expanding tax base, unaware that they are celebrating what defenders of the poor view as "displacement," the reduction of the lower-cost housing stock. Prior residents often cannot afford improvements; many of the real estate interests striving to shape everyone's housing options view poor people as simply standing in the way of revitalization.

Tenants, reacting to such revitalization successes as gentrification, have challenged local policy makers to be more sensitive to tenant needs. Banning condo conversions, controlling rents, and similar local initiatives are often the result. These actions rest on three assumptions that are often false: that existing owners (1) still obtain at least a fair return on their investment, (2) are willing to continue, but (3) ought to be prevented from profiting from excessive housing demand. Such controls generally force the housing supplier to subsidize rental housing further, which cannot work in the long run. Also, measures like rent controls are only respected by owners concerned with their reputations, while the less scrupulous devise ways around them. They often cause decent owners to sell to sleazier interests. Initiatives like a condominium conversion moratorium to cool off a frenzied market can rarely serve as more than a stopgap. Even though such measures ultimately do more harm than good, their political appeal is, nevertheless, hard to resist.

"Grandfathering" the rights of existing tenants to remain for five years, as San Francisco and Oakland have recently done, buys a little time.[5] However, such controls are not a lasting solution either; they only interfere with the response of the rental housing market to current realities.

Life tenure to residents aged sixty-five and over who wish to remain has also been suggested, but such a measure helps only those who stay put. Once such a regulation is in place, elderly tenants would find moving into any other apartment virtually impossible. Owners would henceforth discriminate against renting to any people nearing their sixties.

Marketing the transfer of development rights is another California strategy that links the right to convert existing rentals to condominiums with the production of new rentals in the area. Without substantial new rental housing subsidies and construction, it, too, is an illusion. It simply forces new developments rather than existing owners to subsidize tenants.

Diverting the stock at turnover into new tenure forms for existing residents holds more promise. Traditionally, renting and owning have seemed mutually exclusive tenure options, when in fact tenants could take much more responsibility for maintenance, heat, and utility costs to reduce operating expenses. Tenants taking on janitorial duties and redecorating to hold back rent increases are only a start. Moderate-income cooperatives and condominiums represent new ventures into this middle ground.

Under cooperative tenure each household becomes a shareholder in the entire property rather than owner of its particular unit. Cooperatives for working- and upper-class households became established in some cities like New York years ago, but limiting equity is a new twist. Limiting equity prevents residents from benefiting from appreciation. This would enable another household to move in without paying a fortune when the first moves out, but keeps the latter from being able to buy in elsewhere. This concept also presumes a long-term, fixed-rate, lower-interest mortgage or government subsidy can be obtained. In hot markets, such cooperative interests, even when they have pulled themselves together, are simply outbid by the more affluent or their agents, for whom tax shelter and appreciation hold much stronger attraction. Cooperatives only stand a chance of taking title to multifamily rental stock before markets become too strong, that is, before the motivation to own for security from future displacement has dawned on most tenants.

Selling the stock to current residents also requires a great deal of persuasion because many of these households want to remain tenants. The home-ownership tax deductions have virtually no appeal at their income levels. Furthermore, it is unclear where enough money for down payments and monthly mortgage payments would come from.

Forming limited-equity cooperatives with lower-interest financing is, nevertheless, the type of initiative HUD may seek to encourage because it has promise in particular situations and has already been done with apparent success in some places.

If such cooperatives had been aggressively pursued in the 1960s when 6 percent interest rates prevailed, then much of the current rental ownership turnover at high interest rates could have been avoided. Should interest rates continue to rise to 20 percent and beyond, it would make as much sense today. Cooperative ownership only confers benefits to its group like those that home ownership provides to families at similar income levels. So this, too, is not a broad-scale solution under the current IRS tax structure. At best, thousands of households, not the needy millions, could be aided in this way if given appropriate technical assistance.

Discovering underutilized space in existing resident-owned stock will undoubtedly play a much more important part. Home sharing, mother-in-law, and accessory apartments, and "unsanctioned" income units (discussed more fully in the resident ownership section later) are especially suited to accommodate small, elderly households that until recently have sought traditional apartments.

All these so-called solutions amount to little more than tinkering. Even together they can address the needs of only a small fraction of the tenants increasingly unable to afford decent housing. Ultimately, both the unrealistic tenant expectations as well as the growing, underlying bias toward home ownership in the federal tax code must somehow be faced.

In the 1960s, the mobile middle class simply avoided urban problems by moving out, in effect bequeathing the disadvantaged the low-rent apartments they no longer valued. But in the 1980s, in areas where housing suddenly seems scarce, various classes have begun to compete for what remains available. Income tax incentives now virtually urge all households in the 30 percent and higher tax brackets to own their own residences, exacerbating latent strains within the urban social fabric.

The coming tug-of-war among those with economic interests, those with political strength, and those who cannot afford to move could become serious and unpleasant if mediating institutions cannot reconcile these competing interests into neighborhood harmony. All too easily these issues polarize along class and racial lines. Already some flare-ups and disruptions have occurred. Rental housing enters the 1980s with a legacy of mistrust between income classes generated by expectations that will be hard to change.

New Trends Require New Responses

Conversion of rental stock to condominiums, in spite of front-page publicity, has not yet become the major factor reducing the low and moderate income housing stock in most cities. It is simply a much-publicized new way out for a few owners. Inflation, abandonment, and arson remain the more serious eroders of the low and moderate income rental stock.

Local policies are often unrealistic in their attempts to control rents and discourage sales and condominium conversions, while awarding assistance to politically favored developers without regard for underlying economic realities. In the long run this cannot preserve the housing stock for current residents; it can only erode it or drive it to others able to pay more.

The economic gap between income and expenses must be closed. If tenants will not or cannot pay their current owners more rent or assist in reducing operating costs, then their options diminish daily. It is too late to build enough new housing; sufficient appropriate public subsidies are unavailable. In the short term, the primary policy option remaining to cities is to reduce ownership turnover as much as possible and to treat the long-term owners already there with much more deference. Their low-interest financing or outright ownership is an important asset. Rewarding decent owners for housing long-term tenants and encouraging them not to sell their properties now, even as rental apartments, to any new owners is the best way to postpone the inevitable loss of these properties as lower-income shelter.

Special incentives to encourage long-term owners to continue serving long-term elderly tenants include:

- Modest grants to long-term owners upon completion of energy-conserving improvements or upon the refinishing of apartments occupied by long-term residents if they execute a lease. A lien could serve to recapture the grant in the event the property is sold or the households are displaced.
- Raising assessments only upon sale. This would be another effective technique for encouraging long-term owners to continue. Official tax policies frequently prevent this, yet current reassessment practices are often so murky that they actually induce disinvestment.
- A local capital gains tax on short-term or excessive real estate appreciation (over 30 percent per year) to discourage traders, those who speculate in housing futures as if they were commodities. As a bluff this may have symbolic value. It is hard to implement.

Such an about-face, praising long-term owners and ministering to their very real concerns so they will not sell when opportunity knocks, will not come easily after a decade of sharply polarizing media debate about rental housing issues like "slumlords" and disinvestment.

Wherever housing shortages appear serious, the more advantaged seek entry to this stock in one way or another. Local authorities cannot prevent sales, or condominium conversions, any more than they could prevent disinvestment and arson in the past. Current owners will not stand for much more regulation. The most effective safeguard (short of direct ownership by the present residents themselves through cooperatives or as their own condominiums) is to encourage current owners to stay on wherever possible until the surge of new households seeking resident ownership finds more constructive ways to settle down than by displacing the less advantaged.

Clarifying the uncertainties and red tape confronting current owners and managers can also help. Such issues as future property taxes, credit availability, rent regulations, eviction controls, and moratoriums on conversions are all concerns lingering from the 1970s when investor owners were treated as slumlords. Addressing these concerns will not remove all the incentives to disinvest or convert, but it will buy some time to develop broader assistance for tenants and deal constructively with home-owner tax deductions.

Private real estate interests that jointly served to provide most rental housing in the past have often come to expect the worst from local government. Now they either seek escape or act in ways that only hasten deterioration of the multifamily stock. Much of the blame for this situation falls on past government policies devised during a period of unrecognized slack demand. Procrastinating now, or acting without a broader understanding of the changing market forces, can only compound the rental housing predicament.

Policy Inferences

An improved understanding among local interests of the causes of speculation and disinvestment would enable more appropriate interventions to emerge. Maintaining the stock so that decent rental housing continues indefinitely is still a valid housing goal, but evidently it will not be easy to attain through any means currently within reach of policy makers. Underlying market forces now encourage disinvestment and deterioration even alongside reinvestment and speculation. It may seem hard for local officials to avoid making matters worse. Past local policies can be faulted for having responded too readily to tenant demands. However, representing so many votes, they could not be ignored.

Tenant needs are often a very subjective matter. Many feel entitled to stay in large dwellings yet cannot afford rent increases. Naturally they seek rent freezes or subsidies like Section 8 to enable them to remain. But this does not mean that promising them what they ask solves matters. Simply controlling rents is likely to be counterproductive. Giving assistance to a few in ways that cannot be extended to all who are eligible raises false expectations.

Past concessions compounded problems. In many areas during the 1970s, there was "excess capacity," a hidden surplus of rental units. Rehabilitation subsidies to only the most deteriorated properties destabilized the situation further. Abutting owners held back even more on maintenance to also obtain subsidies. At the same time, the trades and services inflated their charges to all on the basis of what they could obtain from the assisted owners.

Intervenors must consider and anticipate the reactions of all affected interests before intervening to avoid making matters worse in the long run. Avoiding any further counterproductive interventions would already help. Removing inappropriate regulations already on the books can often buy considerably more time for tenants to remain, but this requires a better grasp of rental economics. It is useful to review more closely what went wrong. Market realities became obscured when the relationship between income and expenses became too unpredictable.

"Excess capacity" was not universal. The balance between supply and demand varied locally and changed with time. The smartest housing investors had already noted that the "baby-boom" population began overflowing universities during the late 1960s. Seasoned real estate investors bought where students, two and three together, were pooling their housing budgets to pay much higher rents for units formerly housing families or elderly tenants—a little-recognized precursor of displacement today.

Rental ownership types became much more diversified as sophisticated investors prospected the existing stock for increased rent potential here and tax-sheltered negative cash flows there—passing the dross to unwary newcomers. The potential of converting to condominiums to sell to newly formed baby-boom households is only the latest twist.

Neighborhood context—whether local demand for the stock is seen as rising, stable, or declining—has emerged as a critical shaper of these housing actions, differentiating various types of owners. For example, rising market prices often reflect not the value of the stock as rentals but buyers' intentions to convert to condominiums. Yet rising values were sometimes used by tax collectors to justify increased assessments on all rental stock. In effect this "taxed" multifamily rentals into conversion to condominium tenure, diminishing the amount of lower-income rental stock.

Table 3.2 shows various investor types. The entry of a new type into a local market indicates a change in investor outlook or market climate that policy makers must understand.[6]

Speculation resulted when income outstripped expenses, drawing in less beneficial owners, the traders, and shareholders. Subsequently, when expenses climbed faster than income, other even more pathological ownership styles appeared, including operators, distressed property handlers, and subsidized "rehabbers." In such flux, even responsible interests eventually bow to economic realities and sell to those who can profit, whether arsonists or young condominium buyers. Local regulations usually failed to address the root of the problem: uncertainty obscuring the market incentives. Instead, such interventions usually made matters worse.

Various owner types like slumlords are easily mistaken as the cause of a particular market climate, when in fact they are symptoms; they only signal market change. Their visible actions frequently confound the market, but they are not the primary cause.

The local policy challenge is to understand and correct market imbalances and imperfections. Many stabilizing actions can offset the destabilizing forces signaled by the various owner types. Once the underlying forces are understood, remedies become clearer. The solution lies in obeying a deceptively simple but far-reaching housing policy principle that is usually violated in responding to symptoms: *the public welfare is best served when the relationship between income and expenses in investment properties is neither obscured nor altered in seemingly capricious ways by government policies.* Any measure that increases complexity and reduces predictability must first demonstrate to all interests that benefits outweigh the potential

TABLE 3.2
Various Investor Types Owning Multifamily Housing

Type A *Established Owners/Managers (Blue-Bloods)*
  Like stable markets
  In business a long time for steady returns
  Integrity, pride in waiting list of tenants
  Objective: steady earnings = f(quality, steady services)
  Careful selection of choice, qualified tenants
  Tend to have relatively low mortgages or own outright

Type B *Blue-collar Investors*
  Promote stable markets
  In business for their own (or survivors') financial security
  Unsophisticated
  Objective: equity to cover old age
  Minimize mortgages, own outright if possible
  Tend to cluster holdings near their own residence
  Always on hand to do repairs on weekends, evenings
  Easily and unwittingly overwhelmed by changes
  Ill-equipped to deal with complexity of rent control, housing court, tax abatements, etc.

Type C *Traders*
  Speculate in rising markets
  Seek leverage and rapid appreciation of equity
  Objective: reap gains from appreciation upon resale
  Increase gross rent and capitalize on it by selling at a favorable price
  Tenants incidental; there only to keep building occupied and to demonstrate rent potential to next investor
  Minimize personal exposure (put in little time or money to maintain property)
  Concentrate on cosmetics that would increase resale price
  Polarized tenant-landlord relationships likely

Type D *Operators*
  Derive profits from operations in weak market areas where no one else will supply housing—the low end of the housing spectrum
  Stereotyped as the slumlord, around since at least 1960s
  Can't be dislodged because of problem of relocating tenants
  Objective: high annual returns (attendant high risks)
  Will pay taxes only as advantageous but counting on "end game" (4–5 years before city forecloses)
  Accept and pocket whatever they can of rents obtained
  Minimize taxes and maintenance outlays
  Acquire without conventional mortgage, perhaps take over existing mortgage or obtain mortgage from seller

TABLE 3.2 *(Continued)*
Various Investor Types Owning Multifamily Housing

   Properties may be encumbered with second mortgages, liens, etc.
   Virtually no tenant selection exercised, more likely than most to take welfare referrals to avoid vacancies
   Often own "worst" housing in neighborhood, causing abutters to despise them, seek their removal
   Tenant-landlord polarization
   Likely to be in or get into tax delinquency

Type E *Shareholders*
   Attracted to housing as investment opportunity
   Professionals pool money to invest; form limited partnerships
   Buy at "favorable GRM's" and hope to make money through tax advantages—shelters, artificial losses
   Have limited grasp of housing issues, and responsibilities (other than economic), but may retain a competent management team which is a critical element in delivery of decent housing services

Type F *Rehabbers and Developers*
   Work in recycling neighborhoods and renewal areas
   Often flourished under federal assistance and now have enormous appetite for more subsidies, and/or tax breaks
   Adept at complex problems, handling red tape
   Politically shrewd, often manipulative to the extent of shaping administration of regulatory agencies
   Make their money at front end, ownership incidental
   Shapers of new market trends
   Likely to derive special advantages from tax collection and rent control system
   Increasingly the envy or model of other entrepreneurs

Type G *Special Forces (Distressed Property Handlers)*
   Specialize in newest gimmicks, take over where others leave off
   Always one step ahead of any regulatory agency (municipal, government, IRS, etc.)
   Profits are losses and losses are very profitable
   Calibre of management team, if such exists at all, depends on owner's view of what will return greatest profit within his limited time frame

SOURCE: Rolf Goetze, *Understanding Neighborhood Change: The Role of Expectation in Urban Revitalization* (Cambridge, Mass.: Ballinger Publishing Company, 1979). Reprinted with permission.

drawbacks. All the familiar policy tools must be reexamined in this new light: rent controls and subsidies on the income side and measures such as taxes and code enforcement on the expense side. Any of these may have unanticipated side effects. (See table 3.3).

Local policy must seek to balance between excess supply and excess demand to curb either disinvestment or speculation. For example, a weak market signals excess capacity. Here it is dysfunctional to attempt to control rents and mandate repairs while adding more subsidized housing. A strong market signals excess demand. There it would be foolish to demolish structures that could be repaired by private interests. (In a weak market, demolition makes more sense than boarding up.)

For years it was assumed that any and all deterioration could simply be treated with more subsidies and government regulations and that inadequate funding somehow explained continuing blight. To be effective, local policy must become more sophisticated. It must differentiate between disinvestment caused by insufficient demand, and speculation brought about by too much demand. Local policy must countervail against market imperfections.

In a market stabilized by enlightened government policies, the relationship between income and expenses again becomes more visible to

TABLE 3.3
Local Policy Must Countervail between Extremes

	Too Much Demand	Demand = Supply	Too Little Demand
Symptoms (Causes?)	Rising market	G	Declining market
	Speculation	O	Disinvestment
	Excess demand	L	Excess supply
	Raving press	D	Bad press
		E	
Indicators	Traders	N	Operators
	Income > expenses		Income < expenses
Corrective Remedies	Decrease income	M	Subsidize rent w/o stigma
	Raise expenses	E	Abate taxes
	Control rents	A	Boost neighborhood image
	Raise taxes	N	
	Enforce code		

SOURCE: R. Goetze (1979). Reprinted with permission from *Building Neighborhood Confidence: A Humanistic Strategy for Urban Housing*, copyright 1976, Ballinger Publishing Company.

owners, lenders, and investors. When local checks and balances properly act on the housing system, rewarding those with better properties, neighborhood homeostasis can be maintained. Housing markets now increasingly veer from disinvestment on the one side into speculation on the other because public policies compound rather than check the demand/supply imbalances.

Defining the Rental Housing Challenge

Imperfect markets and ill-considered public policies produce slumlords, but as yet these interests actually own little of the stock. To set out as if all investor-owners were greedy slumlords to be curbed is counterproductive. Much rental housing could survive a while longer and even improve under more enlightened public policies. Encouraging current owners to continue to serve their long-term tenants was suggested as the most effective way to buy more time for the existing rental stock, until basic issues like tenant expectations and home-owner tax deductions can be reconsidered. There are neither appropriate subsidies nor new owner types nor even new tenure forms that can equitably serve current tenants nearly as well as most past owners continue to serve them. Making the policies governing apartment operations more open, explicit, and across-the-board would substantially ease their lot as well as improve the behavior of many of these apartment owners. Nevertheless, opportunities to sell or get out of apartment ownership that were absent during the 1970s have emerged and promise to increase sharply as credit again becomes available at acceptable terms.

Displacement, the involuntary replacement of current residents by another more advantaged class, promises to become the most pressing housing issue of the 1980s, because it is no longer possible to add sufficient new housing in desired locations. In preparation for dealing with the space competition, the roles of tenants, owners, and the public sector in maintaining their apartments will need careful reexamination. Residents must prepare to shoulder more of their actual housing costs or consume less housing if fairer new public subsidies cannot be found. If public policy is ineffective in safeguarding the interests of current residents, the more advantaged will simply move in, and the public clamor for action will rise and further restrict the range of options open to local policy makers. As more properties are traded or converted, it will become more and more difficult to slow down and shape the turnover process toward the greatest public good. Now is *not* the time for innovative sounding but simplistic new programs. Instead one must reconsider the expectations, rights, and *responsibilities* of current residents who wish to retain their apartments, as well as the impact that past housing policies have already had on the many owners of this important one-third of the nation's housing.

There is no persuasive evidence of a general shortage of *rental* housing in the 1970s. Rather, in many places renters were "unable to find dwellings of the size and quality they have come to prefer at rents they are accustomed to paying."[7] Now, tenant expectations must adjust.

The cumbersome public sector must be streamlined to enable all interests to understand and respond to the new realities. Since existing housing is becoming more valued, policy makers must learn how to sensitively manage expectations and demand pressures so that cash flows again become adequate to restore housing but not so rich as to provoke speculation and inflation in property values. Developing this sensitivity may be the biggest challenge policy makers have ever faced. Easing the complexity, reducing the uncertainties, encouraging existing owners to stay on, and harnessing the new demand—all make conserving the multifamily stock quite possible. Dwindling federal assistance only underscores the fact that in the next decade the decisive actions must be initiated at the local level. Ultimately this will involve a national housing policy debate about the interrelationships between rental housing and home-owner tax deductions (examined in chapter 4), but in the meantime there is much that can be done at the local level to buy more time for tenants.

RESIDENT-OWNED HOMES IN CHANGING MARKET DYNAMICS

Single-family homes in suburban subdivisions have been the dominant form of new construction since World War II. Like buying a new car every three to five years, moving up to a new home commensurate with the family's status was long considered by most people as a fixed element in the American dream. However, the auto industry went into shock as Americans began to keep their cars longer and then replace them with more energy efficient imports. A new American V-8 no longer serves to express status. The home building industry seems in for a similar shock. Housing is more complex, but status-conscious consumption of brand new housing played an important role in maintaining annual production at two million dwellings during much of the 1960s and 1970s, instead of maintaining and improving existing housing to avert so much disinvestment and abandonment. As with cars, more is now wrong with home building than simply excessive interest rates. Builders seem unable to supply a better model at current financing terms than most people who bought in the past already have, reducing traditional "upward mobility" or "filtration." In fact, the majority of home owners could not afford to buy their own residence were it on the market today.[8]

It seems that those now entering the market, often pooling two incomes, must settle for less in status terms than their parents—a phenomenon already dubbed "downward mobility" by the media. As more home owners stay put, adapting existing housing to changing needs is becoming a many-faceted growth industry. At the same time, new home building is in difficulties. Gas-guzzling, obsolescent cars were more easily replaced than rebuilt. Properly sited and soundly built housing, however, even if worn, can be refurbished and lasts indefinitely. In many instances, particularly in settled areas, fixing up an old house is even better than buying a new one. With new cars better gas mileage has been a major selling point, but newly built homes do not have sufficiently lower maintenance and heating expenses to justify their higher acquisition costs.

The long-term, below-market, fixed-interest-rate mortgage, running at least another ten years, "locks in" many current owners. This now reduces traditional turnover and filtration, as discussed in chapter 2. To sell means giving up that mortgage, a "cost" no new home could match through any potential operating cost savings. Those newly embarking on home ownership, who used to obtain the hand-me-downs, are suddenly the only new home seekers, and they are less able than ever to pay for the new models.

Meanwhile, larger older homes must be weatherized to reduce heating and cooling costs. At the same time, wherever family members leave home, their space can be adapted to new uses. Existing owners can obtain permits for such renovations much more easily than builders can for new developments. Today, delays in obtaining new construction permits only compound the builders' problems of meeting high interest costs before developments can be sold. But the resident owner can, if necessary, bide his time and hide his work. When the permit is issued, he can supervise the quality of the work or do as much of it himself as he wishes, circumventing both shoddiness and the surcharge for a general contractor. Paying union labor costs would add even more, so the enterprising home owner can save up to 40 percent.

Neighborhood Market Dynamics

Chapter 2 outlined how an excess housing supply situation became transformed during the 1970s, through changes in demography, energy use, and inflation, into one of too much housing demand. These shifts in housing demand did not impact all regions equally, nor all neighborhoods uniformly. The rise in the tide of housing demand is much stronger in growth areas and even there, blight and deterioration continue to be problems only less frequently. The new challenge lies in promoting neighborhood stability and revitalization without displacement. At 1970s consumption rates, there no longer seems enough desirable housing to go around, increasing everyone's feeling of being locked in. In fact, there are plenty of residential square feet, making housing really more of a distribution problem. Perceptions and expectations play a major role in this problem deserving elaboration because conventional wisdom is often at odds with new realities.

As yet there has been little research on how neighborhood stability can be monitored and maintained. It is generally not even really defined. Yet without this sensitivity, public interests seeking to revitalize neighborhoods are confused by conflicting objectives: maximizing housing choice, fixing up houses, promoting integration, housing the disadvantaged, or improving the property tax base. Failure to rank these in some order of priority underlies the circular housing debates. Other issues fall into place, if one accepts that the primary role of public policy should be to build neighborhood stability by matching supply with demand. To stabilize neighborhood dynamics, then, requires strategies to countervail against unbalancing market tendencies. Forces causing too much demand here and excess supply there must be understood and redirected.

Housing condition alone is not a sufficient criterion for understanding neighborhood change. Left to themselves, even superficially similar neighborhoods now tend to evolve in different ways, a recent trend not detectable statistically before the mid-1960s.[9]

Local market perceptions, the future expectations regarding housing demand and property values in the neighborhood, now strongly influence levels of maintenance and offers upon sale. In *rising* markets the number of households who seek to live in the neighborhood seems to exceed the available dwellings. In a *declining* market, there is excess capacity; only in a *stable* market do supply and demand balance out. Whereas the costs of maintaining the upgrading are simply a function of conditions, the motivations to fix and improve depend on *perceptions* regarding the future strength of housing demand. Only at market extremes where there is housing abandonment (declining) or conversions (rising) do these imbalances reach general awareness. However, whether investing in upgrading pays rests on *subjective* judgments that influence owners to invest in one area but not in another even where actual conditions seem similar. Excessive demand is "too much of a good thing" since properties rent and sell even without proper upkeep.

Combining the objective housing condition dimension with the subjective market dimension results in a matrix, as shown in figure 3.1.[10] Some cities, notably Boston, have attempted to classify and follow neighborhood evolution on this basis, confirming that perceptions tend to shape future conditions. Furthermore, some regions of the United States (Sunbelt) are more upbeat about housing appreciation (some even excessively so) while others generally have too little demand to induce proper maintenance. This shifts everything to the left or right in figure 3.3. Note that simply classifying

FIGURE 3.1
The Matrix of Housing Dynamics

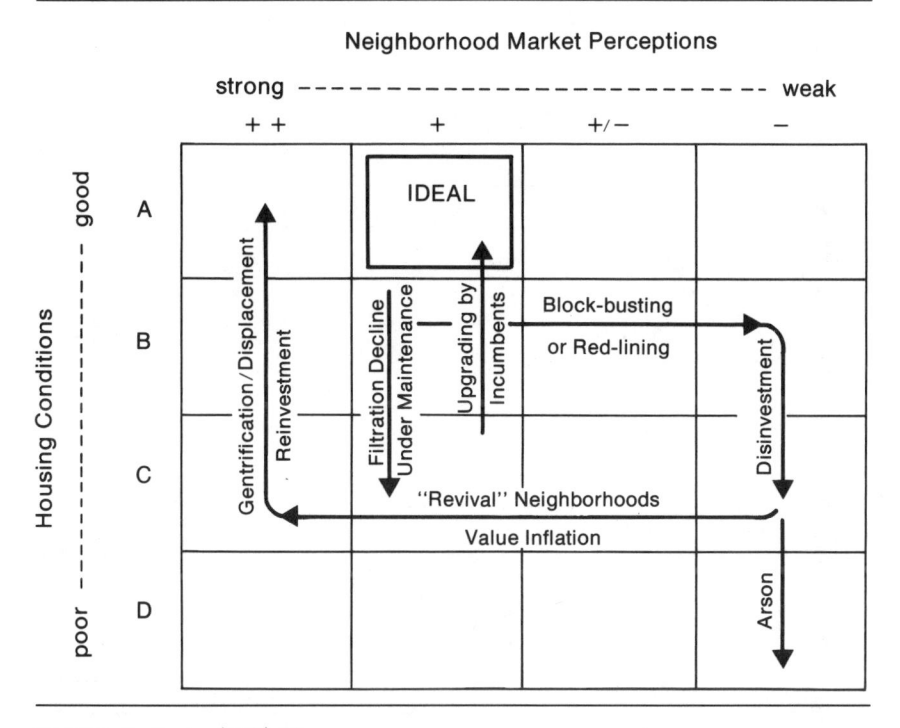

[Figure: A matrix with "Neighborhood Market Perceptions" on the horizontal axis (strong to weak: ++, +, +/−, −) and "Housing Conditions" on the vertical axis (good to poor: rows A, B, C, D). The "IDEAL" box is located in row A at the "+" column. Arrows indicate: Gentrification/Displacement and Reinvestment (upward on left); Filtration Decline / Under Maintenance (downward) and Upgrading by Incumbents (upward) in the middle; Block-busting or Red-lining and Disinvestment (downward on right); "Revival" Neighborhoods / Value Inflation (arrow across bottom); Arson (downward at far right bottom).]

SOURCE: R. Goetze (1979): 38.
Reprinted with permission from *Understanding Neighborhood Change*, copyright 1979, Ballinger Publishing Company.

all neighborhoods on one continuum from good to poor, identifying five stages of decline, as many cities attempted at HUD's suggestion in the mid-1970s, ignores the leading role played by perceptions.[11]

Subjective neighborhood data are now regularly collected on the residential appraisal form that is becoming the standard industrywide introduced by both the Federal Home Loan Mortgage Corporation (FHLMC) and the Federal National Mortgage Association (FNMA). The FHLMC/FNMA Form 70 is increasingly used by lenders so they can resell mortgages on the secondary market. Each time a buyer seeks financing, an appraiser now also evaluates the surrounding neighborhood. (See figure 3.2.) Property values are classified as *increasing, stable,* or *declining;* Demand/Supply is judged as *shortage, in balance,* or *over supply;* and Marketing Time is

FIGURE 3.2
The Standard Residential Appraisal Report: FHLMC Form 70

RESIDENTIAL APPRAISAL REPORT

File No.

To be completed by Lender

Borrower ______ Census Tract ______ Map Reference ______
Property Address ______
City ______ County ______ State ______ Zip Code ______
Legal Description ______
Sale Price $ ______ Date of Sale ______ Loan Term ______ yrs Property Rights Appraised ☐ Fee ☐ Leasehold ☐ DeMinimis PUD
Actual Real Estate Taxes $ ______ (yr) Loan charges to be paid by seller $ ______ Other sales concessions ______
Lender/Client ______ Address ______
Occupant ______ Appraiser ______ Instructions to Appraiser ______

NEIGHBORHOOD

Location	☐ Urban	☐ Suburban	☐ Rural
Built Up	☐ Over 75%	☐ 25% to 75%	☐ Under 25%
Growth Rate ☐ Fully Dev.	☐ Rapid	☐ Steady	☐ Slow
Property Values	☐ Increasing	☐ Stable	☐ Declining
Demand/Supply	☐ Shortage	☐ In Balance	☐ Over Supply
Marketing Time	☐ Under 3 Mos.	☐ 4–6 Mos.	☐ Over 6 Mos.

Present Land Use ___% 1 Family ___% 2–4 Family ___% Apts. ___% Condo ___% Commercial
___% Industrial ___% Vacant ___% ______
Change in Present Land Use ☐ Not Likely ☐ Likely (*) ☐ Taking Place (*)
(*) From ______ To ______
Predominant Occupancy ☐ Owner ☐ Tenant ______% Vacant
Single Family Price Range $ ______ to $ ______ Predominant Value $ ______
Single Family Age ______ yrs to ______ yrs Predominant Age ______ yrs

	Good	Avg.	Fair	Poor
Employment Stability	☐	☐	☐	☐
Convenience to Employment	☐	☐	☐	☐
Convenience to Shopping	☐	☐	☐	☐
Convenience to Schools	☐	☐	☐	☐
Adequacy of Public Transportation	☐	☐	☐	☐
Recreational Facilities	☐	☐	☐	☐
Adequacy of Utilities	☐	☐	☐	☐
Property Compatibility	☐	☐	☐	☐
Protection from Detrimental Conditions	☐	☐	☐	☐
Police and Fire Protection	☐	☐	☐	☐
General Appearance of Properties	☐	☐	☐	☐
Appeal to Market	☐	☐	☐	☐

Note: FHLMC/FNMA do not consider race or the racial composition of the neighborhood to be reliable appraisal factors.

Comments including those factors, favorable or unfavorable, affecting marketability (e.g. public parks, schools, view, noise) ______

SITE

Dimensions ______ = ______ Sq. Ft. or Acres ☐ Corner Lot
Zoning classification ______ Present improvements ☐ do ☐ do not conform to zoning regulations
Highest and best use: ☐ Present use ☐ Other (specify) ______

	Public	Other (Describe)
Elec.	☐	______
Gas	☐	______
Water	☐	______
San.Sewer	☐	______
	☐ Underground Elect. & Tel.	

OFF SITE IMPROVEMENTS
Street Access: ☐ Public ☐ Private
Surface ______
Maintenance: ☐ Public ☐ Private
☐ Storm Sewer ☐ Curb/Gutter
☐ Sidewalk ☐ Street Lights

Topo ______
Size ______
Shape ______
View ______
Drainage ______
Is the property located in a HUD Identified Special Flood Hazard Area? ☐ No ☐ Yes

Comments (favorable or unfavorable including any apparent adverse easements, encroachments or other adverse conditions) ______

IMPROVEMENTS

☐ Existing ☐ Proposed ☐ Under Constr. No. Units ______ Type (det, duplex, semi/det, etc.) Design (rambler, split level, etc.) Exterior Walls
Yrs. Age: Actual ______ Effective ______ to ______ No. Stories ______
Roof Material ______ Gutters & Downspouts ☐ None Window (Type): ______ ☐ Storm Sash ☐ Screens ☐ Combination Insulation ☐ None ☐ Floor ☐ Ceiling ☐ Roof ☐ Walls
☐ Manufactured Housing
Foundation Walls ______
☐ Slab on Grade ☐ Crawl Space

BSMT.: ______% Basement ☐ Outside Entrance ☐ Concrete Floor ☐ Floor Drain ☐ Sump Pump ______% Finished
Evidence of: ☐ Dampness ☐ Termites ☐ Settlement
Finished Ceiling ______
Finished Walls ______
Finished Floor ______
Comments ______

ROOM LIST

Room List	Foyer	Living	Dining	Kitchen	Den	Family Rm.	Rec. Rm.	Bedrooms	No. Baths	Laundry	Other
Basement											
1st Level											
2nd Level											

Finished area above grade contains a total of ______ rooms ______ bedrooms ______ baths. Gross Living Area ______ sq.ft. Bsmt Area ______ sq.ft.

INTERIOR FINISH & EQUIPMENT

Kitchen Equipment: ☐ Refrigerator ☐ Range/Oven ☐ Disposal ☐ Dishwasher ☐ Fan/Hood ☐ Compactor ☐ Washer ☐ Dryer ☐
HEAT: Type ______ Fuel ______ Cond. ______ AIR COND: ☐ Central ☐ Other ______ ☐ Adequate ☐ Inadequate

Floors ☐ Hardwood ☐ Carpet Over ______ ☐ ______
Walls ☐ Drywall ☐ Plaster ☐ ______
Trim/Finish ☐ Good ☐ Average ☐ Fair ☐ Poor
Bath Floor ☐ Ceramic ☐ ______
Bath Wainscot ☐ Ceramic ☐ ______
Special Features (including energy efficient items) ______

ATTIC: ☐ Yes ☐ No ☐ Stairway ☐ Drop-stair ☐ Scuttle ☐ Floored
Finished (Describe) ______ ☐ Heated
CAR STORAGE: ☐ Garage ☐ Built-in ☐ Attached ☐ Detached ☐ Car Port
No. Cars ______ ☐ Adequate ☐ Inadequate Condition ______

PROPERTY RATING

	Good	Avg.	Fair	Poor
Quality of Construction (Materials & Finish)	☐	☐	☐	☐
Condition of Improvements	☐	☐	☐	☐
Room sizes and layout	☐	☐	☐	☐
Closets and Storage	☐	☐	☐	☐
Insulation—adequacy	☐	☐	☐	☐
Plumbing—adequacy and condition	☐	☐	☐	☐
Electrical—adequacy and condition	☐	☐	☐	☐
Kitchen Cabinets—adequacy and condition	☐	☐	☐	☐
Compatibility to Neighborhood	☐	☐	☐	☐
Overall Livability	☐	☐	☐	☐
Appeal and Marketability	☐	☐	☐	☐

Yrs Est Remaining Economic Life ______ to ______. Explain if less than Loan Term

FIREPLACES, PATIOS, POOL, FENCES, etc. (describe) ______

COMMENTS (including functional or physical inadequacies, repairs needed, modernization, etc.) ______

FHLMC Form 70 Rev. 7/79 ATTACH DESCRIPTIVE PHOTOGRAPHS OF SUBJECT PROPERTY AND STREET SCENE FNMA Form 1004 Rev. 7/79 identified as *under 3 months, 4–6 months,* and *over 6 months*. Since this appraisal form is used to grade these mortgages for resale as mortgage-backed securities, an appraiser is unlikely to be unduly positive or negative in his ratings—they reflect the *subjective* neighborhood perceptions at time of sale rather closely. Each appraisal report also has a photo of the property and street scene attached, which becomes more useful as time passes and the actual property changes.

FIGURE 3.3
Assistance Strategies for Neighborhood Revitalization

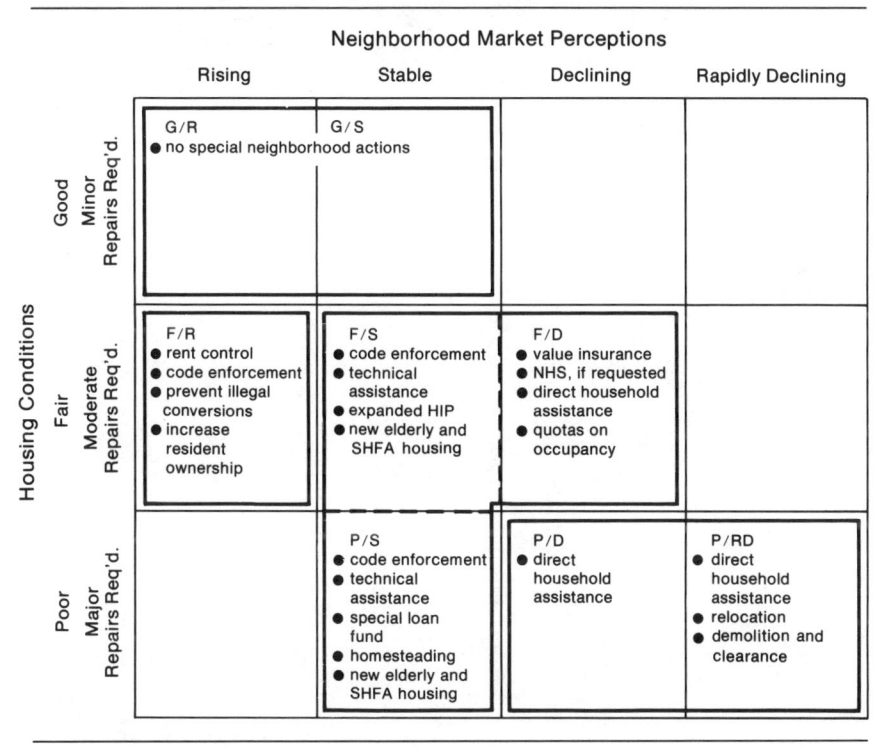

	Neighborhood Market Perceptions			
Housing Conditions	Rising	Stable	Declining	Rapidly Declining
Good / Minor Repairs Req'd.	G/R ● no special neighborhood actions	G/S		
Fair / Moderate Repairs Req'd.	F/R ● rent control ● code enforcement ● prevent illegal conversions ● increase resident ownership	F/S ● code enforcement ● technical assistance ● expanded HIP ● new elderly and SHFA housing	F/D ● value insurance ● NHS, if requested ● direct household assistance ● quotas on occupancy	
Poor / Major Repairs Req'd.		P/S ● code enforcement ● technical assistance ● special loan fund ● homesteading ● new elderly and SHFA housing	P/D ● direct household assistance	P/RD ● direct household assistance ● relocation ● demolition and clearance

SOURCE: R. Goetze (1976): 45.
NOTES: G/R = Good/Rising, etc.
HIP = Housing Improvement Program, typically involving loans, grants, and technical assistance.
NHS = Neighborhood Housing Services.
SHFA = State Housing Finance Agencies, which typically provide below-market-interest loans.
Reprinted with permission from *Building Neighborhood Confidence*, copyright 1976, Ballinger Publishing Company.

TABLE 3.4
The Golden Mean Diagram: Stabilizing Neighborhood Dynamics

Neighborhood Market Types	Rising (Gentrifying) ++	Stable Or Ideal	Declining (Disinvesting) −
Symptoms Indicators (or Causes?)	Excess demand Price inflation (real or anticipated) Speculation Strong press image Immigration of higher class Investment purchases Conversion of marginal space into more dwellings	G O L D E N	Excess supply Uncertainty in property values "Redlining" Negative press image Departure of the able Discretionary sales Increase in low down payment and/or governmental-insured lending Increase in absentee ownership Rising tax delinquency Property abandonment
Corrective Remedies	Dampen outside demand Assist disadvantaged to remain Enforce code Prevent illegal conversions Reassess only upon sale Control rents if necessary Construct additional housing	M E A N	Boost neighborhood image Value insurance for resident owners Improve jobs and income without stigma Support NHS if requested Demolish excess housing (or mothball) Land bank vacant lots until stable

SOURCE: Rolf Goetze, Kent W. Colton, and Vincent F. O'Donnell, *Stabilizing Neighborhoods: A Fresh Approach to Housing Dynamics and Perceptions* (Boston: Boston Redevelopment Authority), November 1977.
NOTE: NHS = Neighborhood Housing Services.

Detecting market shifts as well as actual changes in property conditions over time thereby becomes possible. By allowing local officials to identify subtle shifts in market strength between various neighborhoods, local interests can countervail and help balance market dynamics, as suggested in table 3.4. With such data, officials can begin to separate effective from ineffective interventions. To assist a weak neighborhood, are new sidewalks, more low-interest loans, or boosting neighborhood image more cost-effective—if all cannot be provided? In a revitalizing neighborhood, how long should assistance be provided before recovery is self-maintaining? Viewing each neighborhood regularly through appraisers' eyes would dramatically improve local planning. However, the data on FHMLC Form 70 are not public records. Cooperation between private institutions and the public sector will be necessary to share this information.

The volume of information is quite manageable. Typically some 5–10 percent of the residential properties sell annually. Boston, with a total of 240,000 dwelling units, has 100,000 parcels averaging some 7,000 annual sales. Monitoring neighborhood change through this "window" would be feasible if the accompanying appraisals were shared with local researchers. Lenders are justified in collecting these data because they are needed to grade the mortgages for resale. Residents would have to understand that explicitly identifying market dynamics is the first step toward improving local policies, rather than simple redlining or greenlining in self-fulfilling prophecies as in the past.

Neighborhoods in various cells of this housing condition–market perception matrix respond differently to the same policy interventions. For example, strong code enforcement is usually appropriate and effective in rising neighborhoods, but counterproductive in a declining neighborhood. In a declining neighborhood, assistance directed to all eligible households could help, but in rising markets these might fuel housing inflation by providing even more demand than the neighborhood could handle. Basically, public policy must not only help match supply with demand but often also deal with distorted market perceptions. As a start, table 3.4 outlines some countervailing strategies for rising and declining markets. The astute reader will note parallels to the rental housing situation, table 3.3. Appropriate responses tailored to actual neighborhood dynamics arise from improved local understanding.

Figure 3.3 provides an overview of local actions suitable to the various cells in the housing condition–market perception matrix. Differentiating and coping with differing perceptions are more important than precise classification of particular areas. However, it is useful to briefly discuss some ways for treating stable, declining, and rising market areas.[12]

Tailoring Strategies to Local Neighborhood Dynamics

In stable markets where housing is in good condition (G/S in figure 3.3), no special local housing actions are required beyond appropriate routine public improvements, city services, and equitable shares of general citywide housing credit and services. Where areas are still stable but now require moderate fix-up (F/S), technical assistance, housing code enforcement, and possibly property tax incentives linked to repairs will usually maintain stability and improve conditions. Stable areas needing major repairs (P/S) often require additional government or private sector support such as special bank loan funds, federally assisted rehabilitation loans, or a homesteading program if they are to be restored to good repair. As long as neighborhood housing demand holds steady, such programs have a fairly good chance of success, but an entirely different approach is required if the market is declining.

In declining markets strategies for assistance must visibly increase their attractiveness to boost housing demand. People feel that decline is caused by forces they cannot fight: curtailed availability of regular lending and insurance; fear of lower rental incomes or more problems accompanying new residents; concerns about racial change; and, as the self-fulfilling trend continues, visible deterioration, accumulating debris and trash. Those who see housing primarily as an investment—both absentee property owners and banks—are inclined to overreact at the early stages of decline. Fearing deteriorating property values, they quickly begin to disinvest, curtail maintenance, and extract what they still can out of their properties.

Many residents are forced to remain because they cannot afford to move or sell, but they also begin to undermaintain. Others do sell to new interests like absentee owners, communes, or minorities previously excluded by social norms or stronger prices before the area slipped. As soon as appraisers, real estate brokers, and lenders become aware of the changing situation, the stage becomes set for disinvestment and abandonment that is hard to turn around. Media sensationalizing about neighborhood changes only discourages residents all the more.

Any effective fight against decline must first deal with the market perception of the area. This usually depends on initiative and promotion from within the neighborhoods. Attempts to save a declining neighborhood solely through government action from the outside generally fail unless demand is boosted to match supply. The attitudes of residents are key variables shaping its *perceived attractiveness*. Whether these residents then stay or move is important because others thereby judge the attractiveness of the area. Declining areas can turn around, but the assistance must focus on the households, providing them choices. Will the most capable local leaders stay and promote the neighborhood, or will they flee? City services and the strategies previously discussed for stable neighborhoods can prevent decay only in neighborhoods that already have regained confidence in their own future through increased demand.

If efforts in declining neighborhoods are to be successful, direct household assistance to all eligible residents of declining areas may be necessary. If many move out, taking the assistance with them, that should be accepted. Section 8 housing production assistance, the past treatment for such areas, is counterproductive if it fails to enhance them. Such aid does more harm than good when residents see it as "locking them into projects." Direct financial assistance instead, in the form of either housing allowances or income supports and coupled with job training and counseling, gives priority to helping households. The focus in declining areas, then, must be on neighborhood image and aiding the household, not the housing. Changing market perceptions and demand involve much more than simply providing greater government assistance for physical improvements. They involve the residents, present and future, in ways that open up choices. This is a critical departure from past treatments for deteriorating housing, which increased supply, diverting the remaining demand.

In rising markets the public posture must in some ways be the opposite of that for declining market areas. Rising areas are too attractive, so demand must be "cooled." In such areas, speculatively inclined owners are tempted to reap the gains of rising market values without any improvements in services. Inspection at time of sale and proper code enforcement on those who sharply inflate rents can help encourage responsible ownership.

As shown in figure 3.3, appropriate neighborhood strategies for Fair/Rising areas include special emphasis on code enforcement, monitoring and legalizing conversions, and widening ownership options for previous tenants. Enabling tenants with limited incomes to stay poses challenges wherever repairs are required amidst a strong market demand. Should the tenants be allowed to remain in substandard dwellings? If not, how much of the improvement costs should be passed on to them? At present not enough direct assistance is generally available. Creating condominium options may offer promise for some present tenants by enabling them to become owners and thus share in the rising market instead of being displaced by it. However, few people recognize how easily a rising market becomes too much of a good thing, leading to unfamiliar problems like arson to force out lower-income residents.

General Strategies

Several points should be underlined. *First, public policy must be designed to increase confidence in the future, not simply to underwrite fix-*

up costs. Helping residents boost neighborhood image is appropriate wherever housing demand is slack in the face of a tight regional housing market. Without replacement residents to fill the vacancies occurring through natural turnover, any neighborhood quickly becomes blighted. In some no-growth cities there may not be enough housing demand to go around even as the baby-boom generation settles down. New, assisted development here on cleared land is likely to be counterproductive. The market is the best agent to identify the least desirable areas, but public priority should be given to aiding residents of these areas with special housing assistance vouchers or relocation assistance.

Second, a housing restoration program must distinguish between strategies that are designed to help people and those that improve housing in a neighborhood. For example, in a rising market, private forces may assure the upgrading of the physical stock, but the needs of the residents being forced to relocate must still be addressed.

Third, neighborhood strategies must be formulated within a broader citywide, statewide, and nationwide housing policy context. Certain elements are essential to almost all programs; only their application must vary. These include adequate credit; equity in property taxes; reorganization and reorientation of city agencies (such as code enforcement agencies) toward serving the housing consumer; improvement in the delivery of housing services; availability of public funds to inject at the margin to stimulate confidence; and development of better partnerships between public, private, and community efforts.

In summary, strategies differentiating neighborhood dynamics can only do so much. Frequently, housing change is really only a symptom of deeper problems involving resident incomes and employment. At this point, improving understanding is more important than simply increasing assistance. In many areas, however, once the dynamics are grasped by the many interests now acting at cross-purposes, much improvement can result from even very limited new resources *in concert*. It is important to recognize that in a world that has become so complex that misleading perceptions govern, strategies must be tailored to neighborhood dynamics. What may prove effective in one area may be counterproductive in another. Without such differentiation, confusion increases, only compounding the problems.

Other New Challenges and Opportunities for Local Planning

In many areas perceptions now lag behind a reality sharply altered by demography, inflation, and energy prices. Financial paybacks on housing maintenance and upgrading have long been uncertain, but many urban areas still contain unrecognized housing opportunities. These areas should be marketed to restore housing demand. There are also two particular actions

Apartments, Homes, and Projects   71

providing owners sure and substantial paybacks: weatherization and creating accessory apartments within existing structures. These merit further discussion.

Marketing to Boost Neighorhood Confidence. Too many urban home owners concluded that further investments in their properties would not pay back, as urban issues like busing and redlining dominated the media throughout the 1970s. As complexity grew, perceptions increasingly shaped housing behavior. In Boston, to balance the traumatic news about abandonment, crime, busing, and arson in the mid-1970s, city staff successfully marketed positive neighborhood ambience through creating community posters and broadcasting resident enthusiasm in the media under a HUD-funded innovative program grant. This attracted more college-educated households to consider urban living. Thereupon longer-term residents, seeing people with other options select neighborhoods like theirs over suburbs, began to reconsider home improvements. Changing the negative perceptions induced a lot of fix-up without calling for a great deal of public resources.[13]

In many cities during the 1970s, certain urban neighborhoods were "rediscovered" without any city action.[14] Because of strong stigmas linked with older neighborhoods in the public mind, the newcomers frequently christened their new-found areas with untainted, positive new names such as Park Slope, Society Hill, Queens Village, and Ashmont Hill. Some cities, notably Pittsburgh with its municipal Neighborhoods for Living project, even developed sensitive neighborhood image building into an effective urban planning tool.[15]

Boosterism can easily come under fire now for causing gentrification but, in cases where demand is weak, it can avert continuing disinvestment. Each newcomer induces many more incumbents to reconsider their housing situation. Such marketing is very appropriate wherever market perceptions are unduly negative. However, in areas where the market is already strong, care must be taken to prevent real estate interests from structuring demand for their own ends.

Energy conservation provides quick paybacks. It is a truism that energy costs have soared, but the implications are just emerging. Heating oil in 1981 cost eight times what it did ten years ago, $1.20 instead of $.15 per gallon. Natural gas has quintupled, from $.14 to $.70 per therm. In cold winter regions too much housing built before 1975 now simply "leaks energy like a sieve." Unweatherized dwellings that could be heated for $200 annually in 1970 now cost $1,600 for oil (or $1,000 for gas) to heat as before. (See table 3.5)

If no efforts to conserve heat in these dwellings were made, heating over five years would call for an extra $7,000 *per unit* for oil ($4,000 for gas). Many households, particularly tenants and the poor, not knowing how to do

TABLE 3.5
Energy Conservation Incentives and Potential Savings (per dwelling)

	Annual 1971 Heating Bill Was	Annual 1981 Heating Bill (heated as before) Would Be	Annual Weatherization Incentive	Potential Five-Year Weatherizing Savings
OIL	$200	$1,600	$1,400	$ 7,000
	400	3,200	2,800	14,000
	500	4,000	3,500	17,500
GAS	$200	$1,000	$ 800	$ 4,000
	400	2,000	1,600	8,000
	500	2,500	2,000	10,000

SOURCE: Prepared by R. Goetze from local Boston utility rates.

any better, have simply lowered their thermostats and are still billed more than they can afford. However, these same costs can be viewed as an incentive to insulate and weatherize the stock that pays back in several years—an investment that often provides a better than 25 percent annual rate of return. For home owners, this is a direct payback; for tenants and landlords with leases, it is more difficult to sort out.

In Boston, for example, the typical two- or three-family frame houses built pre-World War II can be insulated for $3,000. This investment alone can save $1,000 annually for oil, already paying back in three years in energy savings (a 33 percent return). As energy prices rise, the payback period shortens and other conservation measures also become attractive. Insulating a dozen such structures generates a man-year of local work, since such weatherization is unusually brain and labor intensive. The materials cost very little.

In general, frame stock is easy to insulate, yet in Boston it was observed in 1980 that 10 percent of such structures still had no storm windows or attic insulation, and 75 percent lacked proper wall insulation. As a rule, the poorer the residents, the more heating dollars simply leaked away.[16] Energy distress is quite regressive. The Boston Redevelopment Authority estimated that, if some $98 million could be advanced for weatherization, reduced energy expenses would return this amount in fuel cost savings in less than four years and at the same time generate 6,500 man-years of local, mainly blue-collar, employment. If such a local weatherization program were created, Boston could gain 2,000 jobs lasting several years and improving the United States' international balance of payments by millions of dollars.

Left uninsulated, the extra resources required to heat this stock in coming years slips right out of the local economy (with virtually no local jobs-multiplier effects) directly to foreigners, just as the heat itself escapes. Already in cities like New York, foreclosures of such two-family homes for nonpayment of taxes or mortgages are way up because of these soaring heating costs,[17] yet too many public assistance programs help poor people pay their fuel bills as if the crisis were temporary.

Weatherization is one issue where public sector interests clearly parallel tenant and landlord interests. Everybody in the area gains from weatherization. If interests that are frequently polarized cannot join together effectively around this clear-cut issue, they certainly will find insoluble the more complex issues like setting appropriate rents or agreeing who should own property in revitalizing neighborhoods.

ACCESSORY APARTMENTS AND HOME SHARING: UNTAPPED HOUSING OPPORTUNITIES

Using surplus space to shelter additional people is not a new idea. A wide range of uses, from taking in boarders to building on the back lot, were common practice in the past. Zoning, however, attempts to regulate such uses. Home sharing, mother-in-law, or accessory, apartments, and granny-flats are frequently mentioned now along with "adaptive reuse" of nonresidential structures. "Unsanctioned income units" is the latest term for some of these new developments within existing housing.

Granny flats are an Australian concept of simply adding a self-contained portable unit in the backyard for the owner's mother. Taking in the mother-in-law but separating her to achieve some privacy, and home sharing (providing space to a live-in renter) are informal responses to local housing needs.[18] Nowadays, however, people seek a clearer definition of their rental status.

Adding new rental units within existing homes provides quick and substantial returns, but can easily antagonize neighbors who fear such conversions might undermine their property values. When one's home is not only shelter but represents lifetime savings for retirement, one cannot be too cautious. Nevertheless, as already indicated, there is tremendous potential for converting underutilized rooms, attic, or basement spaces into additional efficiencies, studios, and mother-in-law apartments. Already many illegal conversions have been made. "Onesies turning into twosies," in George Sternlieb's phrase, are becoming a significant response to unmet housing demand. Typically the individual home owner, no longer using the basement recreation room, wet bar, or children's rooms upstairs, invests $5,000 to 15,000 (often even less) to carve out a new dwelling yielding $4,000 annually in extra income. Usually this not only pays back in well under four years, but it also provides more than economic benefits. Patrick Hare, a Washington-based planning consultant, identifies six potential benefits "for everybody."

- Inexpensive, small apartments for both young and old households seeking rental housing
- Rental income for older home owners
- Security for older home owners from fear of criminal intrusion or personal accidents when alone
- Incidental inexpensive personal services for rent reductions by tenants who have no overhead or travel costs
- Companionship
- A way for older home owners to stay comfortably in homes they would otherwise have to leave[19]

Such conversions are becoming very prevalent in strong market areas, even more than most residents realize. In suburban Boston, the first converters, defying local zoning, served to "test the ice." Others soon followed, circumspectly making sure the abutters would not complain to local authorities. Often nonrevealing building permits—"basement structural repairs, new bathroom"—are tailored to mask the real intent, to avoid reassessment. Usually, care is taken not to alter outside appearance. In many ways, such conversions are a natural response, a kind of safety valve, wherever housing pressures become too strong. However, if they pay back too well, the local assessing and zoning officials must deal with the issue before the process snowballs.

Because accessory apartments virtually everywhere are still illegal, the trend is far below its potential and statistics are unavailable. Nevertheless, as mentioned in chapter 2, possibly up to a half a million additional units have been created annually out of existing, resident-owned housing in strong market areas in years when the housing crunch was greatest. Such conversions involve know-how, up-front cash, and zoning. Many elderly homeowners who now wish to tap their nest egg have the cash; know-how is becoming available, and each deals with the zoning issue individually.

Hare has pondered the zoning aspects for some time and expects those who would benefit from changing single-family zoning in many areas to soon outnumber those who would prefer to see it left as is. Figure 3.4 by Hare suggests how regional housing needs change by "aging" the 1970 demographic profile of a rooted suburban population, the Nassau-Suffolk (Long Island) region of New York. Hare also notes "A recent survey by the Connecticut Department on Aging showed that 75% of the elderly live in households of two persons or less and that 71% have homes of five rooms or more."[20] In many regional housing markets, only a modest annual rate of conversions would serve to meet emerging housing needs.

FIGURE 3.4
Changes in Suburban Housing Needs with Aging, 1970 to 1980

At the same time, parents of that generation are left with more space in their homes than they need.

1970 1980

1970 1980

Population

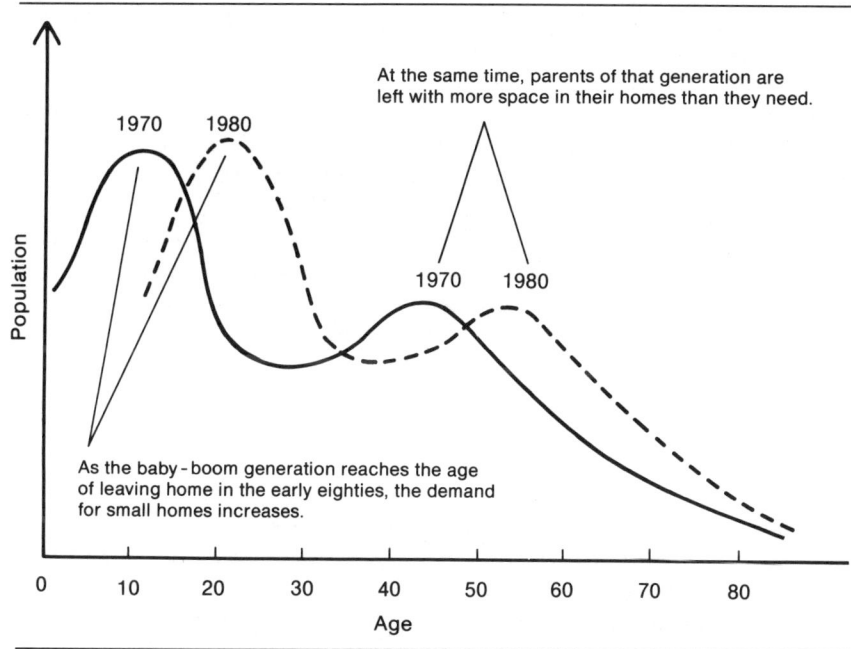

As the baby-boom generation reaches the age of leaving home in the early eighties, the demand for small homes increases.

0 10 20 30 40 50 60 70 80
Age

SOURCE: Patrick Hare, "Rethinking Single Family Zoning: Growing Old in American Neighborhoods," *New England Journal of Human Services*, Summer 1981, p. 34. Reprinted with permission.

In 1978 the Boston Metropolitan Area Planning Council (MAPC) endorsed regulating accessory apartments and proposed a model by-law for this purpose, but as yet few cities and towns in the area have done little more than raise the issue.[21] In 1981, around metropolitan Washington, D.C., where conversions are proliferating but still generally prohibited, the Metropolitan Washington Council of Governments (MWCOG) also proposed legalizing accessory apartments as a housing strategy. It is too soon to judge the response because only a handful of jurisdictions, predominantly mid-sized towns in the Northeast (plus Portland, Oregon), have enacted ordinances permitting accessory dwellings.[22]

The MWCOG report, after surveying fourteen jurisdictions allowing accessory apartments in single-family homes, identifies some further public benefits linked to legalizing such apartments. Accepting that they are going to happen anyway, the MWCOG report concludes that local control would provide safer housing, better upkeep and upgrading and would also increase property values, thereby boosting local property tax revenues without raising everyone's taxes.

The MWCOG report does not mention that illicit and untaxed conversions often benefit the actual converters significantly more. To impose regulations now and increase property assessments may raise strong resistance on the part of converters. Yet not adopting regulations and not reassessing seems unfair to all the abutters without conversions, who gain no rental income and may even experience a relative loss in their property values on account of their neighbor's conversion.

Community debates to legalize accessory apartments hinge on subjective interpretations of who actually gains and who loses—and here the media once again play a major role in framing the issues and shaping perceptions. "Carving up the American Dream" implies that accessory apartments are bad and authorities should prevent them, while "New Housing Boon as Empty-Nesters Share Their Homes" suggests a positive new trend. Unfortunately negative coverage on this issue already predominates in the trend-setting *New York Times*.[23]

Municipalities do face a major challenge in devising constructive ways to handle this divisive housing issue. They will have to be both open and sensitive in deciding how to channel the extra income from these apartments. How much should remain with the home owner; how much is to be taxed away? How will property values of nonconverters be affected, and how should they be assessed? What should be done about nonconforming conversions that are already occupied?

Fundamentally, excessive housing demand in attractive locations produces these effects upon home owners locked in and reluctant to move to smaller dwellings. Accessory apartments challenge local jurisdictions to render Solomonic judgments on such unanticipated issues. The elderly, particularly the home owners, are the main constituency able to raise the issues and press localities for a satisfactory solution.

CONDOMINIUMS AND COOPERATIVES: NEW TENURE FORMS

The introductory chapter suggested that the most pronounced housing clashes are likely where existing rentals are being converted to sell to the more affluent, displacing and even "trashing" old residents. Single-family neighborhoods may gradually pass to higher-income owners, but selling multifamily stock to new residents involves much more dramatic and visible shifts. "People will rent crap, but they won't buy it," has long been a real estate maxim. To sell stock, like old apartments, lodgings, and single-room-occupancy (SRO) hotels, requires developing new appeal.

In areas where housing seems suddenly scarce, this new appeal quickly arises from location, the security from future displacement, the chance to tax shelter income, and the lure of appreciation. These all now enhance ownership of housing stock easily ignored by the better off a few years ago. The condominium conversion process typically starts with the luxury stock, but once the local market for this new tenure form is established, anything nearby, even SRO hotels, may be drawn into the conversion process. Inflation and dwindling of both new construction and direct federal housing assistance brings out the unexpected strength of home-ownership incentives embedded in the federal tax system. But these are blunt tools spurring revitalization that easily cause speculation because they so strongly favor the affluent. As previously stressed, the same dwelling "costs" the affluent much less than it *actually* costs a household making too little to take deductions.

Wherever supply shortages appear imminent, housing *now* seems worth hoarding—an unfortunate pattern only exacerbated by bans on future condominium conversion and rent controls. Whether occupied housing is rented, owned as a condominium, or even owned by one and rented out to another has profound implications for its future. Much housing that could have continued serving as cost-effective shelter has instead become converted to a speculative commodity for profit and appreciation, to be paid for by higher carrying costs and through tax breaks to the more affluent. Only suggestive data are available on the tendency of the affluent to stake out many more square feet of housing, but undoubtedly this is becoming more pronounced.

Scarcity causes three basic American rights to collide in multifamily housing: (1) the right to a decent, affordable home, (2) the right to gains, tax shelter, and appreciation, and (3) the rights of residents to remain in their communities as tenants. Housing shortages force one of these rights uppermost—and if reasonable people cannot resolve the conflicts, the political process will proceed without regard to the consequences.

Now, wherever it seems too little new rental housing can be added, apartments still affordable to the working class (and provided until recently by the private sector at a profit) are being converted—to be simply taken over by the more affluent at substantial gain to the converters. It seems absurd when U.S. Steel, instead of making steel, tries to buy up an existing oil company, inflating its value by using tax credits provided by the Economic Recovery Tax Act of 1981. This condominium conversion process is even more counterproductive, forcing elderly residents to move out with little warning while converters speculate for the affluent, and HUD, the government agency in charge of federal housing policy, equivocates.

Diluted in national statistics, the conversion process may still be largely invisible. HUD reported in 1980 that only 1.3 percent of the rental stock had been converted, as if that were reason to relax.[24] Just before a plane crash both vehicle and impact area would also appear normal, particularly if both cannot be seen in the same picture. However, the time for action is early, before too many options are lost. The Griers observed in 1981:

> For some kinds of people, in some situations, the probability of displacement is much higher than [our study] suggests. We can conjecture that it approaches 100% for certain groups—like elderly tenants on fixed incomes in apartment houses slated for conversion to condominiums, black low-income renters in inner city neighborhoods being "gentrified," or rural homeowners in the path of highway construction. Moreover, no statistics can adequately reflect the pain and anxiety of those facing displacement.[25]

Under current tax laws the financial attractiveness of converting for the affluent is so great wherever there are housing shortages that little can be done locally to stop the conversion interests once a new market for condominiums becomes well established. Fortunately that is still a few years away in most areas, but in some, the best "easy pickings," up to one-quarter of the suitable multifamily stock, already have been converted.[26]

Already abuses by the biggest converters like Invsco, branching out from success in Chicago, have become the target of congressional inquiry.[27] At these hearings, Leon Pastalan, a gerontologist, noted:

> Many of the studies found that the first 3 months immediately following the move are the most dangerous in terms of increased mortality rates, and other serious illnesses and other adjustment problems. So basically, if we are going to intervene with any sort of help, it really needs to be done immediately prior to the move and post-move. After 3 months, it tends to be probably a bit late.

Pastalan closed his testimony with a poignant quote from a Catholic sister: "You know, I don't know a gardener in the world that would transplant an 88 year old tree."

"Mom and Pop" converters who handle no more than ten dwellings at a time may seem unkind when they refuse to renew leases of long-term tenants, but larger transactions involving several hundred units at once are bound to disrupt a tight housing market much more traumatically. Furthermore, such large converters are also easy targets for community organizers.

Banning further conversions simply drives the various interests pursuing their "rights" further apart. Tenants dig in their heels about conditions in fighting rent increases; investor-owners of worn rental properties become reluctant to continue low rents once they glimpse the bail-out that conversions can provide; and those who already own condominiums experience a further windfall as "they don't make them any more" enhances the value of their dwelling. Altogether this only raises conflicting demands to a new pitch.

New development and conversion of appropriately sited nonresidential space help divert excess demand, but often take too long and usually cost more than recycling the run-down rental stock in prime locations. Furthermore, everyone, even the residents, wants his stock improved without displacement.

The challenge lies in devising ways to upgrade the stock without speculatively inflating property values. What can localities contribute toward this goal? Frequently proposed initiatives include encouraging limited equity cooperatives, taxing away excess gains, and granting life tenure to prior elderly residents. However, as discussed in the apartment section, these "fixes" mislead; their effects are limited and often counterproductive.

A direct government subsidy or rent voucher to the disadvantaged would be much more appropriate because the public sector would bear the costs rather than attempt to shift them to housing suppliers. Direct assistance can be effective if, *at the same time*, demand in hot spots could be diffused and redistributed to avoid underwriting speculation.

Countervailing against market extremes again emerges as a critical local function: divert excess demand away from neighborhoods that have become too desirable and toward those where it is weaker, and match regional supply to demand. As long as the underlying federal credit and tax policies remain unchanged, other actions like helping prior tenants become home owners are little more than false promises that increase frustration. Ultimately the municipalities where the effects of these problems play themselves out must form a coalition to work toward more appropriate national policies.

PUBLIC AND ASSISTED MULTIFAMILY HOUSING IN A CHANGING CONTEXT

In some mature cities, close to 10 percent of the stock is assisted. Recently, more and more housing development there required ever deeper subsidies, a trend that could not continue. Even if federal housing commitments are renewed in the future, they are unlikely to develop much more housing under these programs. Nevertheless, assisted housing in general is worth a closer look because many think more money is all that is needed to produce additional units, while others assume the already-built assisted housing will simply maintain itself. In some cities like Boston, one-quarter of the public housing stock is already vacant and uninhabitable. Generally, operating costs on assisted developments are soaring faster than tenants' ability to pay, requiring greater and greater subsidies to avert foreclosures.

Nationally, only around 3 percent of the housing stock, some 2½ million dwellings, were directly assisted through government programs in 1980. This includes not only public housing but also rental units, aided through various federal programs including Sections 221(d)(3), 236, and 202 as well as Section 8. Since many states support housing in ways that piggyback on federal assistance, obtaining more precise totals without double counting is virtually impossible. The details and endless revisions in particular assistance formulas are not worth elaborating upon here: it is the underlying patterns that we must seek to understand.

Many people consider public housing a bargain. Each unit receives at most $200 monthly in public subsidies, less than half the annual taxpayer subsidy for Section 8. However, the $500 per month subsidy in Section 8 developments may more truly reflect the cost of providing decent public housing—$6,000 per unit annually (more than the entire yearly income of some residents). Section 8-assisted residents contribute one-quarter of their annual income, and taxpayers supply the balance, subsidizing up to five-sixths of the actual Section 8 unit costs.

Adding to the assisted housing stock became increasingly costly and difficult even when funds were available. The development process became so labyrinthian with Catch-22s that fewer and fewer albeit larger developers continued to produce. At the same time, operating costs in the standing inventory went out of control. To avert losing what already exists requires diversion of funds initially earmarked to expand the assisted stock.

Heating costs are only one important factor. The home owner now keeps devising new ways to keep from being "nickeled and dimed" and now dollared to death by his heating costs, but assisted housing cannot adapt so responsively. Heat at 68°F is still mandated. In public housing it is hard enough to keep replacing broken windows with Lexan let alone to provide double glazing. Lewis Spence, the court-appointed receiver for the Boston Housing Authority, stresses that public housing is like an obsolete car that gets less than ten miles per gallon—and that the funds necessary to modernize or provide fuel have just been cut off by the Reagan administration. The countless nonprofit church and community groups that were invited to replace slumlords also rehabilitated and developed housing unaware of rising energy costs. As if heating problems were not enough, in many developments adequate security, better management, and removing the stigma of living in "projects" are equally pressing issues.

A Historical Synopsis from One City

A brief chronology places the challenges now posed by assisted housing into perspective. In the 1960s expectations were high that government programs could eradicate substandard housing. Under the Great Society, LBJ's ringing phrase, policy makers debated how the after-Vietnam "peace dividend" could be harnessed, while Congress began to fashion a succession of new housing assistance tools, one superseding another even before their full impact could be grasped.

Boston may be an extreme case, but through understanding its pathology the task ahead can be better defined.

- In the early 1960s, the "housing problem" was seen largely as one of substandardness, to be addressed through clearance, stepped-up production, and rehabilitation, soon called "rehab." Mortgage insurance and below-market financing channeled through nonprofits to circumvent slumlords were presumed to be solutions. Their tendency to mask risks and inflate costs was then not apparent.

- HUD, the newly created cabinet level Department of Housing and Urban Development, sought demonstration sites to show how 221(d)(3) could rehab old housing instead of simply bulldozing it. Secretary Weaver came to Boston and initiated BURP, the Boston Urban Rehabilitation Program, unaware how the sudden fix-up of 2,000 slum units at once would touch off demand for relocation assistance. To empty some buildings for rehab, developers simply let the heat fail.

- Congress became appalled at the visible budgetary impact of 211(d)(3) which, rather than pay for development over time, committed the entire subsidized mortgage amount up front in the first year. In response, Section 236 was designed to provide even deeper subsidies released over the life of the mortgage.

- Around 1970, local concern about public housing segregation and conditions led to a host of well-intentioned remedies including centralizing management, integration, and providing that tenant rents not exceed 25 percent of income, the so-called Brooke amendment.

- The first BURP projects began to have trouble meeting soaring operating costs around 1972, even before the Arab oil embargo, but local rent controls were adopted and interpreted to bar any rent increases violating the spirit of the Brooke amendment, paying only 25 percent of income.

- By the mid-1970s, foreclosures had already forced HUD into possession of several thousand assisted multifamily units (paralleling other problems in HUD single-family programs). These troubled projects were largely rehabs from the BURP demonstration. The first 500 units were resold without subsidy for a giveaway 2.3 cents on the original mortgage dollar, but the losses to the FHA Insurance Fund were so great that HUD began to seek face-saving alternatives.

- Congress and HUD unveiled the three-in-one Section 8 program in 1975 to replace all previous housing assistance programs with yet a heavier subsidy. It also guaranteed qualified owners and developers a steady and adequate rent stream covering low tenant incomes and vacancies.

- After 1976 some Section 8 money was committed to produce new elderly housing as well as to recycle politically important properties, but much was quietly channeled to boost project incomes in earlier developments to avert more financial distress and future foreclosures.

• Nevertheless, by 1979 most assisted rehab projects were in financial distress, requiring transfusions of more and more Section 8. At the same time HUD initiated several simultaneous disposition demonstrations to sell off the HUD-held inventory. Rehabs were repackaged to make geographically more manageable projects while, in new developments, ways of selling to residents were explored. Virtually 100 percent Section 8 commitments upon disposition were provided by HUD to boost resale and thereby avert severe losses to the FHA Insurance Fund. In the words of one observer, "This promises another twenty years of good money to mask initial program failures."

• By 1980, as additional federal commitments were dwindling, the majority were applied to prevent further erosion of the assisted inventory. Meanwhile, Section 8 new development costs per unit were rapidly climbing, and residents in gentrifying neighborhoods began to clamor for assistance to avert displacement. Even had President Carter been reelected, the widening gap between housing expectations and what Section 8 could actually deliver was becoming unbridgeable. Tenants in still-solvent Section 236 projects, paying rents over 25 percent of income, also began to demand more subsidies.

• Developments aided by MHFA (Massachusetts Housing Finance Agency) avoided many foreclosures only by shrewdly skirting the worst situations and more adeptly tapping additional subsidies as operating costs soared.

• Meanwhile, Boston's Housing Court (BHC) had decided in 1976 that Boston's public housing was a disgrace and appointed a Master to remedy the situation. In 1980, frustrated by 25 percent vacancies and lack of progress under the Master, the BHC selected a receiver, Lewis Spence, who immediately mapped out an ambitious modernization program requiring yet more public subsidies, to "invest" $75,000 to $90,000 *per unit*.

Throughout, housing actions reflect the "we can have both guns and butter" mentality. It seems people thought all expectations that sounded reasonable were attainable: improving housing, renewing the city, helping the residents, creating jobs, and reducing housing costs.

Obviously, calls for ever more money and better management must be accompanied by a deeper understanding of what is wrong and what is now possible. The gap between project income and expenses is not solely caused by the assistance programs, but they decisively contributed to creating and widening this gap. The Brooke amendment, while generous, was inequitable and unaffordable without a deeper and more lasting national housing commitment. Compared to the private market, it is much harder for public programs to adapt and respond to changed realities like energy costs and unrealistic tenant expectations. If assisted housing is to remain viable, each tenant's demands and housing responsibilities must be reconsidered.

Public Housing

Something is fundamentally wrong when 4,600 units, one-quarter of Boston's public housing, become uninhabitable in a tight rental housing market. The physical layouts, the lack of security, the social pathology of some residents, the youth vandalism, the economics, the antiquated heating systems, the public housing stigma, the patronage cum civil service management—all are variously blamed, but after fifteen years of controversy there is still no agreement on how each contributes. Digging for some answers is worthwhile because reclaiming these units costs much less than the $50,000–$70,000 now required for each additional unit under Section 8. Here I can only advance some hypotheses.

The status value of living in older public housing sank very low in the 1970s housing glut as anyone who could moved out. At the same time, many new local measures were introduced for integration and centralized rent collection. Unwittingly, the new laws also encouraged rent delinquencies, and counterproductive tenant selection and eviction procedures. All these well-intended interventions inadvertently squelched the residents' sense of control over undesirable tenant behavior. Newly completed elderly projects then often siphoned off the very residents who helped hold youth pathologies in check and stave off such bedlam as retaliatory terrorism and arson as entertainment.

An overall resurgence of interest in urban living makes it possible to:

• improve the status value of public housing in the eyes of its residents, as well as the general public,

• grant residents more control over matters important to them like tenant selection and evictions, and

• rebuild a sense of trust between residents and the administrative staff that should support them.

Such far-reaching changes, however, require revising and rethinking much of what was done in the 1970s. The following must be considered:

• A leavening of more employed and working-class poor is essential. Income limits must be raised. At the same time, idleness of residents rejected by the economy must be addressed.

• Racial quotas as currently applied will continue to be obstacles. Instead, racial balance must be pursued with the active consent of the residents acting through resident tenant councils.

• Projects should be vying for new residents. A better media image will induce others than "last resort" households to apply. The media are likely to prove open and receptive to positive, human interest stories regarding living in public housing, as soon as there is something to be told. And once this happens, the residents themselves will develop a higher regard for their housing.

- The new mix of residents, involving more "deserving poor" as role models, could be a better agent for dealing with problem families, rent arrears, and skip-outs.

- New arrangements of responsibilities between residents and the public housing administration are essential to develop a healthy sense of resident control over issues vital to them. For example, in Baltimore tenants are furnished the paint and are responsible for decorating their own apartments. They cannot use peeling paint as a defense for nonpayment of rent. Tenants there initiate their own clean-up campaigns, police the grounds, print their own regular newsletter containing tips on living in public housing, arrange competitive arts and crafts fairs, rope the youth into talent shows, and so forth. Management can do much more to encourage such initiatives.

Before public housing revives, difficult issues must be addressed: shortage of resources, low resident and staff morale, inept management, the unproductivity of union labor, the racial composition of individual developments, and what can be done about "problem poor" near whom no others will live. However, having a stronger mix of residents will help resolve such currently intractable issues.

Staff morale and performance are often a critical problem area. Under the double protection provided by civil service and union membership, incentives for good performance, sanctions for nonperformance, and accountability appear hopelessly muddled. But the executive right to fire even one person a year, "the one just asking for it," could change this. However essential, providing such power within troubled public housing agencies almost requires an act of Congress.

The vacancies in public housing offer a unique opportunity for experimentation to ease regional displacement concerns. Some projects with extensive vacancies might be recast in the public mind by offering units to able young households like those who pioneered the revitalization of redlined neighborhoods. Releasing 20 percent of the units to the private market could transform whole projects. Such innovations should be matched by an equal number of voucher certificates to enable qualified public housing tenants to obtain other private housing in turn, so the assisted housing total is not reduced.

Annual taxpayer subsidies in public housing are under $2,500 per unit, less than half the cost of subsidizing new Section 8 initiatives. However, public housing can be counted a bargain only when it is properly maintained and fully occupied by satisfied tenants. "Down on the floor you can't fall anymore" summarizes public housing's possibilities. Easing up on heavy-handed public interventions and redeveloping a responsive staff can permit creative new solutions to emerge as renewed overall urban housing demand of the 1980s lifts public housing from its stranded position of the 1970s.

Forces Discouraging New Assisted Development

As new development in mature cities became increasingly dependent on subsidies, this housing assistance masked reality. At the same time that it caused expectations to snowball, it allowed costs of providing and maintaining new rental housing to soar. This is untenable. In 1980 only one of every five households eligible actually received assistance. The outcry about cutbacks from both developers as well as tenants waiting their turn is understandable. However, retaining the assisted stock already built must receive first priority. This requires devising ways to reduce maintenance and operating costs or to increase rent revenues per square foot.

Basically, assisted housing programs have promised too much while fudging true costs. The programs were too complex and involved too many interests. Rising energy costs only made matters worse. As a result, responding to changing realities was even more difficult for subsidized developers than for private rental investors.

When the more complex Section 236 program replaced 221(d)(3), in the late 1960s, the number of developers was radically reduced. In Boston it dropped from hundreds to scores. Section 8 development was yet again more difficult; only a handful continued, each much more sophisticated and larger in scale than before. Another quantum jump in program complexity would stop further assisted development altogether.

Recent development costs are so high because they cover much more than bricks and mortar. They also cover union-scale wages, high-priced impact analyses, and even the rebuttals to challenges mounted by publicly supported community opposition. While tugs-of-war among residents, the developers, labor, and the sponsoring public agencies continue, staff and finance costs run on and on. This process can evolve no further; something basic must change.

Events everywhere are forcing people to become more resourceful and self-reliant. Resident ownership allows much more flexibility: lowering the thermostat, discovering new ways to conserve and keep warm by capturing solar energy, making simple repairs and taking charge of redecorating oneself—even adding accessory apartments. The government assistance programs seem cumbersome and ill equipped to help tenants adapt in similar ways to the changing realities.

It is time to reexamine the roles of tenants and their expectations.

How much total public assistance is likely to be available? Shared equitably, how much is that per household? What are tenant preferences regarding housing types appropriate for assistance? What part can tenants play in maintaining the housing, conserving energy, and reducing overall housing costs? Since the total resources are inadequate, what should receive priority?

The modest resources likely to be provided in coming years cannot enable many more eligible households to attain their expectations, particularly through new development. Instead of recent programs that commit $600 per month per dwelling to a few developers building for a few, a fresh approach is needed providing $120 per month directly to five times as many eligible households under guidelines that improve available existing housing. This aid must also help residents cope with change rather than make them more dependent, as past government assistance has done. Government policy makers dealt directly with developers, supposedly acting on behalf of the tenants. However, this left tenants out of the picture, along with their actual concerns, preferences, and potential contributions. If the growing tensions between expectations and reality are not reconciled, the tenants are the real losers.

Now, while the exceptionally strong demand can still be harnessed, is the time to review all the functions of assisted housing. Some tenants, paying only one-quarter of household income in public housing may view the appalling conditions surrounding their lives as poor recompense for being locked in. Many would prefer safer housing. Some could shoulder more responsibilities, others would accept something like home sharing, and still others would willingly pay more of their income for housing that appeals to them.

Much assisted housing, particularly developments housing the elderly, remains physically in good shape. However, measured against resident-owned housing, operating and maintenance costs are simply rising out of control. Given the inefficient ways public resources have been used throughout assisted housing, some quantum improvements are possible *within existing budgets* under better management.

In spite of concerns about housing shortages, public housing assistance cannot solve macrosupply problems along with everything else. New development is a separate issue. At best, housing assistance can work at the margins, to improve housing maintenance and distribution among those who now compete for it. Vacant public housing, wherever present, is a resource waiting to be tapped to help resolve the twin problems of displacement and too much new housing demand. The greatest promise lies in approaches that redefine the roles and responsibilities of all affected interests, especially the residents, to discover ways to achieve more satisfying results with the available resources.

IN SUMMARY

The private rental housing stock still shelters one out of three households, but many tenants want more housing than they can now afford. In the last decade tenants expanded into an underutilized inventory and often no longer pay their way. Ownership turnover at 1980s financing costs worsens the rental economics.

As housing shortages emerge, this unexpectedly enables owners to convert rental apartments to condominiums. Traditional, lower-cost rentals can only continue if previous owners can be persuaded to remain and not sell. Under current federal tax laws, rental housing will, nevertheless, erode or be converted. The main question is only how fast?

The public housing inventory is also unlikely to expand. The challenge will be to keep it from eroding without providing ever more subsidies. Operating costs are not adequately controlled. Improving management and dealing with wasteful behavior on the part of a small but rough minority will both be essential.

If the rental inventory will expand so little, how will people be housed? More densely than before—and the adjustment could be painful whenever realities are judged against housing expectations of the 1970s.

Rising costs and zoning regulations limit growth of the stock of single-resident-owned homes as well. Excess demand here, excess supply there challenges the public sector to help resolve supply/demand mismatches in order to avert more speculation and disinvestment in stock that is still a bargain to conserve. Marketing weaker neighborhoods, weatherizing and upgrading obsolescent stock, and providing accessory apartments wherever the stock is underutilized promise to be on the 1980s housing agenda.

New housing forms like row-houses, mini-homes, and stacked flats will come to dominate in many new developments. New tenure forms for multifamily stock—such as condominiums and cooperatives—will also emerge, and be appropriate where this is not simply a takeover of existing stock by the more affluent.

Continued new development would have averted only some of these challenges because new life-styles and living preferences have emerged that traditional forms, like the single-family home, would not accommodate. Just as car size and performance have had to adjust, so must housing to smaller, less expensive, and appropriately located units whose operating costs can be readily controlled. The next two chapters discuss the federal and local policy changes that could facilitate such adjustments.

Federal Actions
RESTRUCTURING THE HOUSING SYSTEM 4

SHIFTS IN FEDERAL HOUSING INFLUENCES

Mortgage and credit policies, tax expenditures, and heavy subsidies to some housing suppliers have been the dominant federal influence on local housing markets. Federal initiatives regarding crime, schools, welfare, and transportation are but secondary. Taking advantage of the changing federal influences including the new IRA and Keogh provisions, housing vouchers and revised tax deductions, combined with new direct savings incentives for home ownership, can beneficially restructure federal housing policy.

The Changing Role of Direct Housing Assistance

In December 1981, the Reagan administration's Office of Management and Budget proposed dramatic cuts in virtually all direct housing assistance programs, a proposal unthinkable one year previously. Not only new production but public housing operating subsidies and modernization commitments, as well as funding for troubled projects, housing counseling, and even the Community Development Block Grant (CDBG) and Urban Development Action Grant (UDAG) programs—all direct assistance programs were to be phased out within two years. Regardless of the rate of follow-through, simply raising the possibility suggests how much the assisted housing constituency has weakened. In the early 1970s, when President Nixon attempted to halt mortgage assistance programs, they were soon replaced with Section 8; this time promises to be different.

Trying to buy a little more time and money for some of the past programs is a natural response on the part of the assisted housing coalition, but housing policy is already moving in new directions, consistent with the proposal put forth by the Office of Management and Budget (OMB).

The President's Commission on Housing (PCH) proposed "consumer-oriented housing assistance grants," that is, housing vouchers. In its *Interim Report*, issued October 30, 1981, the PCH stated such grants should replace future commitments to build under Section 8, Section 202, and public housing laws.[1] Furthermore, the PCH recommended that grants go to only very needy, low-income households (those below 50 percent of area median income and paying rent in excess of 50 percent of income or suffering involuntary displacement). Local administration and support systems and payment formulas have not yet been resolved, but the intent is to assist households search out and obtain decent housing without inflating local rental markets.

To improve the availability of adequate housing, the commission made a number of other recommendations such as allowing new construction with Community Development Block Grant funds. Even should these continue, they would produce little additional housing due to high per-unit costs and the necessity of paying total development costs up front (instead of over time as past programs encouraged). The PCH also recommended a number of indirect measures to help housing generally: tapping pension funds as new sources of credit, continuing FHA insurance for segments of the market not adequately served by the private market, extending investment tax credits to cover rehabilitation, and permitting tax-free savings accounts to encourage and assist home buyers save for a down payment. Mortgage revenue bonds, however, both tax exempt and taxable, the PCH felt required further study.

Critics easily scoff that, in effect, these recommendations simply turn the task of housing the poor over to private enterprise and are, therefore, not likely to deliver much, but as yet they have advanced no real alternatives beyond continuing past programs. The current financial context must be considered before supportive federal initiatives to improve housing can be discussed.

How Mortgage Credit Has Altered

Fixed-rate, long-term amortizing mortgages have served to foster resident ownership since the Depression. Over the years the interest rate gradually rose, the term lengthened, and the size of the down payment declined.

In 1970, $140 paid monthly until 1999 still bought a median-priced home with 20 percent down under a fixed market rate mortgage. Chapter 2 elaborated how this "windfall mortgage" explained the soaring appreciation of American homes during the 1970s. In 1980, buyers had to pay $549 monthly to reach what initially resembled a similar arrangement. Soon after that, interest rates rose even more and fixed-rate mortgages became hard to obtain. Current buyers were being asked to compensate lenders for the negative real interest rate they granted the earlier buyers. Home prices then began to falter. Discounts and "buy downs" became dominant price considerations, often reducing effective prices by as much as 15 percent.

"Creative financing" and the various mortgage innovations discussed in chapter 2 were all devised to support the home prices that soared during the 1970s. In the interim, the American home seemed to have become a tax-sheltered collectible, forcing buyers to become much more sophisticated about interest and tax effects.

Wherever housing seems in short supply, scarcity now prices it— and the more affluent have discovered how tax deductions work in their favor. To achieve more equitable and resourceful housing utilization, interest rates must be at a more realistic rate above inflation, and home-owner deductions must be modified. The current situation is too biased toward the affluent.

Tax Expenditure Revisions

Many people naively interpret any tampering with home-owner deductions as a call to simply wipe them out, when in fact they could be beneficially modified, holding past buyers "harmless." Regressive U.S. home-owner deductions, overshadowing other tax-sheltered investments, contributed strongly to the worsening economic distribution in housing, too much for the affluent and those who got there first, too little for the poor and those seeking housing now. Speculative conversions of lower-income rentals to condominiums serving the more affluent illustrate this federal tax effect.

The Economic Recovery Tax Act of 1981 introduced some far-reaching modifications that could ultimately have quite an impact on housing. At this point the changes can only be identified because it is hard to predict how both residents and savers will respond to the revised incentives in the face of future economic trends. Both resident-owned and rental housing, as well as savings and mortgage patterns, will be affected. In spite of internal inconsistencies, several components in the 1981 Tax Act contribute to easing both housing inflation and mortgage interest rates in coming years.

First, everyone can now shelter $125,000 (instead of $100,000) in home appreciation from capital gains taxes, spurring more home ownership and enhancing appreciation.

Second, capital gains tax rates are reduced and investment tax credits are extended to some housing investments, but not rehab. The details are complex, too complex to lay out here, but it would be a mistake to assume that they solve housing problems. They fail to address the more critical issues of maintenance and distribution, but only help production, possibly even encouraging the throwaway mentality. Ultimately, financing and the local housing market remain much more important factors than tax breaks. Other factors being equal, however, these tax policies make important distinctions at the margin between sales and rental housing, and between new and existing stock. They still favor resident ownership and the affluent, in contrast to the third and fourth components.

Third, the reduction of taxes for the higher-bracket taxpayers dulls the incentives driving them to buy housing as tax shelter. The effective advantage of the affluent in mortgage interest rates has been somewhat diminished. Still, a distinct tilt toward the affluent remains, compared to those who take the standard deduction.

Fourth, retirement savings incentives were strongly increased by sheltering them from income taxes. Although indirect, these new savings provisions may be the Reagan administration's most far-reaching housing policy moves to date. The one-year tax-exempt All-Savers certificates, offered through 1982, induced little new savings. Rather, they simply diverted existing funds. However, the much more generous long-term, tax-exempt retirement savings incentives promise to create new savings. The revised IRA (Individual Retirement Account) and Keogh provisions enable owners to put aside and shelter earned income from federal taxes until they reach their sixties and are presumably in a lower tax bracket. This separates out the savings function that many resident owners began imposing on their homes in the 1970s.

Trading up in housing became an increasingly important tax dodge to save up for retirement. Now, instead of employing housing for this purpose, people can deal with financial institutions to tailor more flexible savings programs for themselves, hedged against inflation. And instead of seeking so much mortgage credit to leverage housing appreciation, they will turn savings over to institutions to invest, reversing the recent lack of savings. This helps reduce both the housing demand that was driving up prices for existing housing as well as the mortgage demand that was inflating interest rates.

The Reagan administration has, in effect, brushed past the tangle of direct housing policies, like it or not. Without endorsing the draconian measures OMB has initiated, one must admit that clearing the decks of ineffective, out-of-date programs was becoming necessary regardless of who was elected in 1980 and essential to a fresh start. The 1981 Tax Act provides a promising base for new, less counterproductive housing policies. In fact, the President's Commission for Housing has already tried to look beyond the outcries raised by the cutbacks and identified two important components for a future housing policy: housing vouchers for tenants and assisting savings for home buyers. Modifying tax expenditures is a third component, not mentioned, that would decidedly enhance the effectiveness of a new housing policy tailored to the emerging realities. Spelling out how all these might work together is useful at this point.

FEDERAL INITIATIVES TO IMPROVE THE LOCAL HOUSING MARKETS

Previous chapters elaborated the ways in which private rental housing is at a disadvantage, due largely to the way federal tax deductions enhance condominium and home ownership. National housing policy must now resolve this fundamental bias one way or another. Policy options to aid rental housing ultimately reduce to giving tenants more direct assistance, capping home-ownership tax expenditures, and enhancing other forms of savings besides home ownership.[2] The 1981 Tax Act already moves toward the last, so let us begin by considering the first and second, and then conclude with an even more radical proposal, a savings for home-buying program.

Providing Consumer Housing Assistance Grants

Housing payments were endorsed by the President's Housing Commission in its 1981 preliminary report, but with few specifics. Conceivably, even home ownership could be assisted as proposed below, but let us first focus on assisting renter households.

Housing vouchers as a concept have been seriously discussed since 1937; and in one form, housing allowances, they were the focus of an elaborate $170 million federal experiment that began in 1970. This is often referred to as EHAP (the Experimental Housing Assistance Project).

It is difficult to summarize or even agree upon all that was learned from the EHAP because different components were tested in widely varied contexts and there were many conflicting objectives.[3] The Section 8 program was adapted to test the allowance concept, requiring many compromises. In some settings existing housing authorities were involved, while in others agreements were made directly with landlords. Clearly, housing allowances are no panacea; in fact, many who are eligible are unlikely to participate. However, the voucher concept did seem much better suited to aiding households with the greatest needs, a group poorly served by past programs. There was much less "creaming," which aids only the uppermost among those qualified. EHAP helped many tenants who stayed put, and often augmented their income for nonhousing items, but it promoted less integration or mobility than some supporters wished. The fear that it might inflate local rents, however, proved unfounded in a "supply experiment" part of EHAP.

The voucher system originally proposed in 1971 for New York City by Ira Lowry of the Rand Institute still provides the most appropriate concept in my opinion.[4] In this formulation, household eligibility, local market conditions, and rent-gap criteria are combined to provide a voucher to every eligible household, empowering each to seek its own decent, affordable apartment. Any owner providing such housing is subject to an inspection to certify that the dwelling meets basic housing codes. In the event that the dwelling is substandard and the owner fails to make adequate repairs within a reasonable time, the household's voucher would no longer remain valid for that particular unit, but it could readily be applied to any other dwelling that complies.

Phasing in such a voucher program slowly minimizes rent inflation, prevents administrative overload, and affects the national budget only gradually. The phase-in for eligible households can be achieved over three and one-half years by initially qualifying only household heads with one social security last digit, then every four months another new last digit, selected by lottery.

Even though assistance payments today under the original Lowry concept would probably average $200 monthly (half the average Section 8 unit commitment), total costs on a national scale would, nevertheless, eventually dwarf current housing assistance expenditures because so many more would participate—perhaps five out of ten who are eligible.[5]

Providing $3,000 annually per household (including administration) costs $3 billion per million households. With 5 million participating households, this ultimately adds up to $15 billion. Since the Reagan administration seems unlikely to embark on any new assistance program eventually costing some $15 billion annually, the PCH endorsement must be considered very tentative and for a much more limited "housing payments" initiative.

Modifying Tax Expenditures Further

Providing tax credits and modifying deductions are the principal alternatives for new policy development if Congress is not inclined to provide more direct housing assistance at this time. However, aiding tenants directly through tax deductions to them as renters would have little impact, even though this is frequently proposed. Doing so would also raise the issue of double counting since investor-owners of rental properties already claim these costs in their own tax calculations.

Capping home-owner deductions may not look like rental assistance, but indirectly this aids tenants because it would discourage overinvesting in scarce existing housing as a collectible.[6] Many believe that home-owner tax deductions must be preserved because they make high acquisiion prices and interest rates more affordable to buyers. However, it is more likely that these tax deductions allowed prices and interest rates to rise.

They enabled recent sellers to obtain much higher prices for existing stock, boosting housing inflation wherever housing seemed scarce.

Capping home-owner deductions and limiting them to the primary residence would ease market pressures on the existing stock and keep future housing tax expenditures from increasing by $10 billion every year. An appropriate cap could be set at $12,000 in interest and property taxes, well above the current norm for a median-priced home. It would gradually take increasing effect with inflation, focusing benefits toward the more needy.

Substituting a simple home-owner tax credit for the current system of deductions would be an even more progressive move. An Urban Institute proposal substituting a 25 percent federal tax credit for mortgage interest and property taxes (instead of deducting the full cost of these from pretax income), would be much more equitable and help many benefit from home ownership who currently take the standard deduction.[7] This would require only a simple modification of the Internal Revenue Service's basic income tax form. A direct tax credit of up to $3,000 per home owner would help anyone buying or owning a median-priced home, but prevent the current problem of the affluent outbidding the poor for existing homes.

Under such a capped tax credit, middle- and some lower-income households would also benefit indirectly from lower housing prices, as higher-income households shift investments away from existing housing. Since protecting potential appreciation now underlies exclusionary zoning and much other home-owner opposition to lower-income in-migration, a capped tax credit might also lower resistance to neighborhood changes. Gold can be safely kept in a vault, but housing appreciation has become ever more sensitive to neighborhood reputation and change. As retirement savings become freed from trading in housing, and instead flow directly into IRA and Keogh plans and other investments, residents might again become more accepting of diversity and even welcome other walks of life into their neighborhoods.

Tampering with home-owner deductions has been likened to touching a sacred cow by *The New York Times*, asserting there is deep-rooted resistance to altering them. Nevertheless, rental housing will gradually phase out with existing households unless this fundamental federal tax bias favoring home ownership is either changed as suggested above, or housing vouchers for some millions of renters are introduced.

Creating a Federal "Credit for Home Buying" Program

A third assistance component is a tax-exempt savings program to help more people become home owners. The government should not provide outright down-payment grants or special insurance to buyers without down payments because that circumvents the vital function owner equity plays in housing. Some have proposed that savings in IRAs be withdrawable without penalty for first-time home buyers, that similar Individual Housing Accounts be created with a tax credit for deposits, or that federal grants match savings one to four. As yet, however, these are simply fresh ideas.

A completely separate home savings program that was developed years ago in West Germany can serve as a model. In it federal premiums reward future home buyers for saving under contract within private sector institutions called *Bausparkassen*, a German variant of our savings and loans. Many West German households contract to save regularly (over at least seven years) toward a housing target, called "contractual sum," in accounts earning 2.5 percent to 3 percent interest.[8] Those below median income receive a government premium amounting to 14 percent of annual savings, sharply boosting their yield. These funds are thereby committed to housing. When about 40 percent of the contractual sum has been deposited, the saver becomes eligible to obtain a "building loan," in effect a second mortgage at 4.5 percent to 5 percent interest.

A similar home savings system in the United States could help a half million first-time home buyers every year as well as the home-building industry and lenders at the same time. If Congress could prevent the housing tax expenditure loophole from widening as far as the CBO predicts and explicitly divert some of these tax-exempted billions into a new "credit for home buying" program, it would help all major housing interests, yet simultaneously ease inflation at reduced cost to the American taxpayers. Capping *future increases* in home owner deductions would make this "miracle" possible. A brief outline illustrating a possible U.S. savings for home-buying plan follows.

The lending industry would establish new tax-sheltered accounts similar to IRAs offering a contract savings plan for future home buyers. Lenders would pay 5 percent interest on these savings, but for all who met their annual agreed-upon savings target, the U.S. Treasury or HUD would contribute an additional 10 percent, establishing a swelling pool within the lending industry enabling qualified participants to both save for home ownership and obtain 10 percent home mortgages. Determining precisely who are qualified home buyers and what are appropriate housing types should be high on the national housing policy agenda. Such a new approach is needed now, both to aid first-time home buyers, as well as to help the lending and housing industry avert problems like those besetting the U.S. auto industry.

A $500 federal premium linked to tax exemption might induce a future U.S. home-buyer couple to save $5,000 in the first year. Another $500 in the second year would induce them to save another $5,000, bringing their amount on deposit with the bank at the end of the second year to $11,275 (including 5 percent annual interest). Repeating this would raise $17,339 by the end of the third year. When around 50 percent of the total amount sought for home buying has been deposited, the home-buyer couple can proceed, receiving the whole contractual sum, both their accumulated savings and a longer term mortgage at 10 percent interest for the balance. The lender provides this mortgage from funds that others, in turn, are depositing meanwhile. Thus a federal commitment totaling $2,000 to $3,000 to each future home buyer in $500 annual increments would restore home buying, building, and lending. Figure 4.1 roughs out some first approximations.

Assuming a half million future home buyers enter this savings program each year, $250 million in government home-owner premiums would provide $500 to each in the first year. In the second year, $500 million would be required to also cover the next half million embarking. By the end of the sixth year, when the first half million home buyers would be ready to take out mortgages, $1.5 billion in government premiums would be required annually. From then on, these government premiums would induce $15 billion in new private savings every year from three million home seekers, sustaining a $44 billion pool for making home mortgages at 10 percent.

Many will wonder who would save $5,000 per year. Yet in the past families have invested similar portions of their annual income into their children's education. Saving such amounts toward future home buying certainly represents a shift in approach. Households unable to set aside so much could still participate but would only be eligible for a smaller, below-market mortgage, enabling them to buy a more modest home or finance the balance conventionally. As another alternative, the federal government could also provide even bigger savings incentives, but care must be taken to avoid past pitfalls of creating inequities, raising false promises, and making inflationary budget commitments.

Countless variables are yet to be defined in this new home-savings concept: mortgage terms, eligible housing stock types, tax-exempt status, interrelationships with market interest rates, penalties for early withdrawal, and so forth. However, the basic concept can be developed from previous experience here with IRAs and in West Germany with *Bausparkassen*. Although the actual costs are complex to analyze, the public costs of any such home savings system would be considerably less than leaving housing tax expenditures uncapped.

Such a $1.5 billion new government housing assistance program helping millions become home owners would be far more effective and suited to the times than the past combination of direct assistance programs like Section 8, 312, block grants, and so forth, which together were already costing the taxpayers so much more than that in fiscal 1981. Some $30 billion in tax expenditures should remain, modified as described above, but capping

FIGURE 4.1
An Illustrative Savings Program for Home Buyers

This table demonstrates how one household would accumulate savings for home buying.

Year	Balance from previous year (including 5% interest) +	Deposit +	Government Premium =	Accumulated Balance
1	0	$5,000	$500	$ 5,500
2	$ 5,775	5,000	500	11,275
3	11,839	5,000	500	17,339
4	18,206	5,000	500	23,705
5	24,891	5,000	500	30,391
6	31,910	5,000	500	37,410

By the end of year six, $30,000 of tax-exempt home-owner savings plus $3,000 in government premiums, together earning 5 percent interest, will have generated $37,410 for this home-owner couple, qualifying them for a $70,000 home, to be bought with their savings and a $35,000 mortgage at 10 percent for the balance.

If the first cohort contains a half million such future home buyers, then $1.5 billion in government premiums (over six years) would have induced them to save $15 billion, generating $18.7 billion. Even as these are taken out to buy houses, the next five cohorts will already have accumulated a balance of $44 billion, continually replenishing a pool for making 10 percent mortgages. This perpetuating system enables successive cohorts of home buyers to buy their own homes.

If the government were to provide more subsidies or stronger incentives, home buyers could buy sooner, possibly when they have saved only 20 percent–30 percent of the contract sum. However, care must be taken to avoid past pitfalls: inequities, hidden but massive future public commitments, raising excessive expectations, and so forth. Recent cutbacks by the Reagan administration coupled with the 1981 Tax Act set the stage for such a savings for home-buying initiative.

---

them (so they do not increase by $10 billion each year) would provide much more than the $1.5 billion required annually for this far-reaching new savings for home-ownership program. Capping them could also pay for rental housing vouchers.

IN CONCLUSION

The linkages between perceived housing shortages, prices, rents, local regulations, the federal tax code, and savings are complex and hard to grasp, but that does not mean that doing nothing or attempting to preserve the status quo in these changing circumstances best serves current interests. The intent of the preceding discussion was to raise issues and illustrate some appropriate new federal responses. Modifying tax expenditures, adding housing vouchers and federally rewarding savings for home buying would provide many benefits all around. Together they would not only foster more moderate-income home ownership, but also preserve rental apartments by slowing their conversion to condominiums, free up mortgage money, and shift investor attention to other more productive investments. In addition, they would reduce the call for more counterproductive government assistance to aid the disadvantaged, as well as gradually help balance the federal budget. Of course, many will resist such changes even before they can grasp them or understand their implications. Some recent buyers, sensing that housing appreciation may be diminished by these modifications, may vehemently oppose them. Vocal, influential interests that have come to consider strong housing appreciation as a right have already invested widely, counting on inflation to continue. Solving the housing predicament will not be easy. Rapid housing appreciation and unaffordability are but two aspects of the basic, U.S. housing dilemma, seen from the Have and Have-not sides respectively.

After decades of tinkering to improve housing, it is time to identify and address the underlying forces eroding the viability of the entire housing system. Demographics, new life-styles, energy scarcity are all difficult to alter, but the income tax code and the credit system, products of Congress, can now be constructively harnessed to reshape local housing markets. The most promising federal policies in this belt-tightening era involve a capped 25 percent tax credit for home-ownership expenses, and some improved incentives to save for home ownership combined with shallow housing vouchers to all needy renters so that current owners will continue to serve their tenants' needs:

It will be interesting to observe whether federal policy can alter fast enough to prevent class warfare between housing Haves and Have-nots and to save the "partnership" between existing tenants and current rental property owners. Tenants, landlords, owners, lenders, investors and managers have far more to gain by relearning how to work together under the above initiatives than by muddling along through the increasing polarization and conflict fostered by past policies.

Local Actions to Improve Housing

FITTING AND FINE-TUNING

5

Helping supply match demand geographically and continually is the basic housing challenge. In areas like California, which limit development in the face of rising demand, those already owning housing have benefited while newcomers find entry difficult and the poor fear displacement. Growth controls can seriously distort the basic housing system. In other areas with too much stock, even where abandonment is not actually visible, maintenance does not pay. Inadequate demand or surplus stock discourages everyone, also distorting normal housing behavior.

In many sections of the Sunbelt, however, including Atlanta, Dallas, Houston, and Denver, it seems that rapid growth of supply has equaled demand, while elsewhere a slower growth rate matched demographic changes. Wherever supply and demand are in step, the housing system seems less deranged. Administering local regulations sensibly (like zoning, growth, and rent controls) and decontrolling where appropriate are important to maintaining a viable housing system. Otherwise, like any tool used out of place, these factors exacerbate problems. Citizen expectations and perceptions are also important elements.

Even though the Reagan administration is said to be shifting all action to the state and local levels or the private sector, modifications in the federal tax and credit systems are necessary. Local initiatives can all too easily mask problems, thereby compounding them. Local tinkering, pursued with good intentions but too little understanding, tends to destabilize neighborhood dynamics and further polarize local interests.

Little can be done at the state level beyond playing a supporting, technical assistance role, guiding local actions, and providing the necessary public resources that municipalities generally lack. In confronting and adapting to new realities, it is unwise to simply expand state efforts to cover gaps exposed as federal programs are withdrawn. Such past efforts often compounded the problems.

However, four areas are appropriate for local action to increase the productivity of available resources and help supply match demand: (1) monitoring neighborhood change, (2) reexamining "governance" (the basic rules and payoffs to all actors), (3) dealing with citizen expectations, and (4) reintroducing public assistance constructively. This chapter addresses each of these in turn.

MONITORING NEIGHBORHOOD CHANGE

Since housing often no longer gradually "filters" but "plummets" here and "rises" there, clarifying neighborhood dynamics is essential. Chapter 3 outlined a conceptual approach to understanding such market changes in housing stock and property values, and also proposed that municipalities play a countervailing role to balance out supply and demand mismatches. Table 3.4 summarized the way local roles should be tailored to particular neighborhood dynamics, diverting demand from where it is too strong and boosting confidence in weaker areas.

To allocate public resources effectively and stabilize the local housing situation with its many submarkets requires imparting a more sophisticated understanding to all interests. This calls for a new data and information system differentiating neighborhood dynamics and attuned to reflect year-by-year changes. Various cities have improvised some approaches to these ends. Among the best known are Washington, D.C.'s MAGIS (Municipal Automated Geographic Information System) and Denver's Land Use Information System.[1] These parcel-based systems use central computers to store, retrieve, and manipulate city record data from many sources. If money were no problem, they would be nice to have. They were created during less austere times and cost a lot simply to maintain today.

Since no system has been developed that is fully appropriate to understanding and dealing with neighborhood dynamics, it is useful to lay out the essentials here. Conceptually, such a system must be developed on three levels: (1) a census block-type information system for background; (2) an extensive, citywide parcel-based system for monitoring shifts in neighborhood dynamics, and (3) an intensive monitoring of some five to ten microstudy areas typifying various market dynamics to detect the causes of changes in specific cases. This requires a three-tiered, integrated local information system as outlined below.

The U.S. Census Background System

Even as the 1980 census data become available, they are only very rudimentary because information is aggregated to the block level (to provide confidentiality), presented through cross-tabulations, and gathered only every ten years. Thus change cannot be analyzed in detail. The 1970-1980 interval is also too long to detect the most significant changes at the neighborhood level, like shifts from disinvestment to reinvestment, changes in the rate of turnover, or the resurgence of resident ownership after many years of decline, and so forth.

Nevertheless, the census can provide both a valuable backdrop as well as fresh reference points for measuring change henceforth in such items as population, race, household size, and income on the demand side, and dwelling counts and sizes, rents, values, vacancy rates, and turnover on the supply side.

Traditional methods of census analysis do not require elaboration here. At this background level, the emphasis should be placed on contrasting neighborhood dynamics over the 1970-1980 interval. Examining changes over time in rank, or in deviations from the citywide norm, can be informative. Rents, values, household size, and vacancies should be examined in this manner. Municipalities should obtain the EDP (Electronic Data Processing) tapes to carry out their own analyses rather than be content with the published materials.

An Extensive, Parcel-Based System for Monitoring Change

One comprehensive system should be constructed to integrate existing information, by parcel, focused on monitoring housing patterns and neighborhood change. Frequently, municipal assessing departments have computerized sales and title records by parcel in addition to assessments. Structural fire data and housing-relevant police statistics should be integrated with this tax information, along with engineering or building department data on housing improvements, additions, and demolitions. Some states, like Connecticut, will provide data on all real estate transactions for a modest fee, and often a private corporation compiles sales, transfers, and mortgage data *by parcel*.

Ideally, such data should be geocoded and electronically stored and available for console terminal displays as well as usable for special studies. Citywide norms for values, turnover rates, appreciation, sales-assessment ratios, and so forth should be generated to guide neighborhood analysis. From the above sources, three immediately useful products should be developed:

- A *simple base file* of pertinent data related to each parcel, suitable for at-a-glance review on TV console display. Data for any property should be callable at will to show structure type, number of units, vacancies at fixed times, tenure type, assessed value, last market sale value, and so forth. Too much information clutter is as harmful as incomplete or erroneous data, so care must be taken to assemble a useful base; and if the data cannot be readily retrieved and manipulated, then the system is worse than useless because special interests will use it counterproductively.

- *A paired sales analysis* to monitor value changes over time of all properties sold more than once. Repeat sales of the same property are more useful for monitoring microdynamics than changes in areawide averages. In some areas and for some house types, appreciation will be substantial; for others it will be low as particular property types or areas come into or go out of favor. Sensitivity to these differences is important for policy.
- A monitoring of assessment/sales ratio trends to detect inequities, changes, and contrasts. Local real estate taxes are a significant burden on property owners, and differential impact will contribute to varying local decisions to maintain, disinvest, or reinvest.

Beyond these, several more sets of data that should be integrated into the parcel-based system if the following intensive microarea case studies confirm their usefulness. Annual data on residents and occupations provide one of the best windows for detecting future trends. Many cities had R. L. Polk data, which was recently discontinued. Some, like Boston, compile their own annual listings of all residents by address, age, and occupation. By electronically comparing current with past residents, "who has come" with "who left," sensitive interpretation reveals incipient neighborhood status changes that would otherwise only reach policy makers more slowly through general consciousness. By also comparing resident data with sales and title records, shifts toward absentee ownership (heralding disinvestment) become apparent early enough to intervene effectively.

Property tax delinquency, liens, and recorded home loan credit (usually available from the state bank commission) should also be integrated into this citywide monitoring system, because tax and financing patterns are the most accurate mirrors of the changes actually occurring.

The best judgment of what further data should be integrated into the citywide system develops from intensive monitoring of five to ten study areas.

Intensive Monitoring of Five to Ten Case Study Microareas

"Neighborhood listening" is an approach recently pioneered in some cities like Boston and New Haven. It commences with gathering both objective and subjective data in half a dozen areas, reflecting diverging market patterns. Representative areas containing some two hundred structures are both manageable and informative.

Sound local policies arise from well-grounded understanding of what is actually taking place in submarkets. Assumptions are frequently out of date or simply wrong. To understand cause and effect, continual monitoring of some five to ten such areas should feed back into ongoing policy making. Without it, officials frequently make erroneous judgments, for example, treating a neighborhood on the verge of rediscovery and speculation as if disinvestment were still the key problem, or assuming that a few low-interest home improvement loans are an effective stopgap until more assistance becomes available (when this more often encourages nonrecipients to discontinue ordinary maintenance while they await their turn).

To fully understand the dynamics in changing neighborhoods, these study areas must be closely monitored through both statistical and interview techniques to detect subtle shifts in motivation on the part of residents, potential and actual buyers, sellers, tenants, investors, brokers, and lenders. If residents had more money would they stay and upgrade, or move out and up? Comparative economic data on housing costs and appreciation are specially useful. Contrasts between areas as well as changes over time are both important to detect.

Regularly hearing from real estate brokers, community leaders, and loan officers is a poor substitute because "folk wisdom" and misinformation are so easily passed on. Someone has to do the research to substantiate whether people are really investing or disinvesting and why. This monitoring of "hard" and "soft" data is best coordinated by a single experienced person involved in all policy discussions relevant to community development and housing revitalization. Responsibility should not be diffused among many individuals because understanding arises from careful synthesis of many contradictory impressions. The goal is to go beyond conventional wisdom to learn what actually shapes maintenance and market behavior.

To detect patterns in these microcases, the data are best recorded on index cards and base maps, until interactive microcomputers can handle such analyses. Once appropriate and consistent early precursors of change are identified, however, these should be factored into the computerized extensive, citywide monitoring system. For example, neighborhood listening may suggest that shifts in tenure or the entry of certain occupations herald change. Counting mail boxes may reveal that new demand is producing illegal conversions. Then monitoring such data on each parcel on a citywide basis would be useful to track divergent market dynamics. Since these microcase studies detect the most useful data and most suitable form for incorporation into the extensive, parcel-based monitoring system, they should commence as soon as possible, before the citywide system has become too fixed and firm.

As microcomputers advance and the cost of data retrieval declines, as laser disc technologies promise easier storage and access to photographs and old data files, municipalities will find the benefits of creating an integrated local information system far outweigh the costs. Already the Lincoln Institute of Land Policy (LILP) in Cambridge, Massachusetts, is developing the appropriate hookups and software to utilize mass-produced microcomputers in streamlining local information for monitoring and understanding actual housing change. The hardware—microcomputer, disk drives and printer—costs less than $10,000. The Lincoln Institute provides the software for a nominal fee to any "master users," those who complete one- or two-week training workshops held at the LILP.

Desk-top microcomputers can already handle upward of a hundred characteristics for each property (for example, sales date and price, property description, neighborhood market trends) enabling a local planner to analyze and identify broader patterns and trends. Adding information collected at turnover on the FHLMC/FNMA standard appraisal form to the local Assessor's and Building Department records provides unprecedented insights into actual neighborhood dynamics and prepares local officials for considering "governance," the largely invisible incentives and barriers shaping local housing market behavior.

REEXAMINING PUBLIC INCENTIVES AND BARRIERS

As the forces actually changing neighborhoods become better understood, the importance of the local regulations and customs governing the housing system emerges. Recent studies, particularly by SRI-International in Menlo Park, California, have been examining "governance," the influence of local regulations, tax incentives, revaluation practices, zoning changes, and so forth.[2] Every local issue challenging municipalities today is surrounded by an intricate but little-considered web of rules and payoffs to all the interests involved. For example, owners often allow rental housing to deteriorate for lack of income or to qualify for federal subsidies, as discussed in chapter 3. Growth controls often distort local housing markets as soaring values, not increased supply, result from excess demand.

How can local understanding improve? A self-assessment can lead the way, following a checklist of neighborhood revitalization questions originally proposed by Tom Chmura of SRI. (See figure 5.1.)

Local planning must consider perceived problems and explicitly identify what local government seeks to accomplish, rather than responding politically or trying to spend entitlement resources "appropriately." Consider dealing with an abandoned apartment building. Instead of simply providing Section 8 housing assistance, analyze the situation, weigh the alternatives, implement a response, and monitor the results—fancy terms, but they

FIGURE 5.1
A Checklist of Questions for Redirecting Neighborhood Revitalization

Analyzing the Situation
—How is the neighborhood "system" malfunctioning? As compared to a stable, well-working neighborhood, what actors are not performing their expected roles? Which of the neighborhood's usual "coping mechanisms" has broken down?
—What is the range of city powers and resources available to address this problem? What does local government seek to accomplish?
—What roles can private institutions and community interests play in helping to address this problem?
—Who are the key actors in the neighborhood for this particular issue? How does the city relate to these actors—through subsidies, regulations, taxation, licensing, or provision of infrastructure? Can any of these be adjusted to serve as an incentive/disincentive to help resolve the issue at hand?
—Why is "do nothing" not an appropriate local government response to the situation?

Weighing the Alternatives
—What are the politics associated with any approach being considered?
—Policy analysis is a must. What costs and benefits are associated with each alternative? Who will win and who will lose if a particular approach is chosen?
—How will each of the major neighborhood interests (home owners, tenants, bankers, realtors, insurers, merchants, organizers, and others) be affected by the alternatives? What, if anything, will each be encouraged/discouraged to do?
—Neighborhood diagnosis is essential. What are current neighborhood conditions? How do residents and others feel about the neighborhood? How have these conditions and attitudes been changing?
—How much of the city's motivation for action is that "everybody else is doing it"? How much is desperation—"we have to do something"—a factor? Have these factors discouraged or influenced objective policy analysis in any way?

Implementation Considerations
—How long will it take for the strategy to start working? Are neighborhood market conditions likely to have changed by then? If so, what will the strategy do, given the new market conditions?
—What steps must be taken to implement the approach? What approvals are required? What new "systems" are needed?
—What city agency will take the lead in implementing the strategy? Will it be sensitive to the perspectives of other interests or will it pay attention to agency preferences?
—If, after implementation, the approach is found to have seriously undesirable effects, how easily could the policy be withdrawn or modified?

Gauging the Impact
—What measures of outcome will be used to access the impacts of the strategy?
—What are likely to be the particular impacts of the strategy on the various interests, public, private, and community, in the neighborhood?

continued on next page

Figure 5.1 *continued*

—Once the strategy has made its impact, will the affected neighborhood be made more self-sufficient or more government dependent?

—What would happen in the neighborhood if the strategy was not used and the city did nothing?

SOURCE: Adapted by R. Goetze from "Rediscovering Governance: Using Non-Service Approaches to Address Neighborhood Problems; A Guide for Local Officials," *SRI-International*, Menlo Park, California, February 1980, pp. 77–78.

constructively redefine the issues, completely transforming the planning process. Rather than allowing local officials simply to reach for more federal housing assistance, this approach guides them toward understanding neighborhood market dynamics, thereby obtaining the most benefits from public resources. Abandonment may be a symptom of too little demand and curtailed private lending, compounded by counterproductive city assessment, rent control, and code enforcement procedures that drive out more responsible owners every day. Private lending may have been withdrawn because rental income seemed inadequate; reassessment may only reflect false values based on condominium conversion potential. To then control rents and enforce codes without adding income is futile. These may not be revelations, but rehabilitating a few of the most deteriorated structures with Section 8 subsidies compounds problems when funds are inadequate to help the rest.

Once a city embarks on this new approach to formulate policy, it will have divorced itself from the futile dependence on evermore federal funds and will be able to design its own assistance programs, enabling it to use more effectively the block grant funds it does obtain.

Neighborhood Housing Services (NHS) in many cities developed out of such a joint private, public, and community process reexamining the actions and causes shaping neighborhood dynamics. This forged effective new partnerships to change local codes and zoning, and to deal with negative neighborhood image, inappropriate forms of public assistance, inadequate maintenance know-how, and the like.

Enterprise zones in England are also rooted in the governance concept; they arose out of the belief that excessive regulation and taxation thwart initiative—and that modifying such factors as taxes and minimum wage laws would unleash initiative more constructively than federal grants and subsidies. However, establishing such zones here may prove much more difficult and less appropriate than developing more creative spinoffs from the NHS approach, which originated in the United States.

Dealing with thorny issues like displacement becomes much easier in the context of monitoring *actual* neighborhood changes as described in the previous section. The displacement debate may be fueled by false impressions, exaggerations, local assessing practices, or even simply by fears of reassessment as newcomers bid up everyone's property values. If high purchase prices are, indeed, caused in part by too few properties changing hands, then it is more appropriate to expand housing supply than to reassess all long-term owners on this basis. If supply were more widely matched to demand, excessive prices would drop. In any case, enough Section 8 commitments to hold "displacees" harmless are not available; assessing practices should be reviewed. Perhaps legislative changes treating long-term owners differently from buyers are also indicated. The point is that reconsidering "governance," the local rules of the game, can lead to better solutions.

Allowing accessory apartments and home sharing (discussed in chapter 3) is another new local issue, this one controlled through zoning. It is also well suited to be handled through monitoring and governance. In many areas, underutilized housing space is an important resource that could easily be tapped. In fact, much housing may already have been converted in many jurisdictions. Legalizing this process may now be a much more cost effective way to "increase" housing stock than through new construction.

The basic approach to reexamining governance is similar everywhere, but where it then actually leads is richly diverse, because it is a function of local realities and perceptions. It produces new initiatives that are more appropriate, being uniquely tailored to the local situation in ways no centralized planning or federal program guidelines could ever achieve. One example is Boston's widely emulated Housing Improvement Program, granting owners direct cash rebates instead of cumbersome interest reduction loans through local banks. Federal assistance tended to suppress this creative process of policy formulation, which draws upon insights already present at the grass roots. These are only waiting to be tapped by public officials and private interests through a better understanding of neighborhood change.

DEALING WITH CITIZEN EXPECTATIONS AND THE MEDIA

> When I went to work for the city in 1957, all we were expected to do was to sweep the streets and pick up the garbage. Now, they want us to feed the kids breakfast, rebuild downtown, make the air and water clean, train the unemployed, and who knows what all. And we're supposed to do all that without raising taxes.

So wrote Richard Hage in 1973, long before federal community development block grants (CDBG) came on the scene.[3] Now, as federal assistance is again being curtailed, local officials sense that citizens often expect far more than can be delivered. This calls for examining what shapes these local expectations. In view of the reduced public resources at hand, all local interests must come together to devise more realistic expectations as well as to increase their resourcefulness in meeting them.

A 1980 study, *Dividing the Pie: A Guide to Local Resource Allocation Practices* (the RAP study), sought to understand rather than to evaluate or measure the allocation process.[4] The study penetrated complex procedures local officials often use to handle largely invisible and sometimes taboo subjects like race relations, political mistakes, and citizen expectations. Its main findings were that cities seemed to have had remarkably different experiences with CDBG. Some stressed revamping their downtowns, some worked conscientiously with neighborhood groups, while others were aiding gentrification by simply marketing neighborhoods to newcomers. These local activities were often superficially impressive, yet few really seemed to know how to pursue or recognize restored vitality. Some municipalities were attempting to help "people"; others were seeking to improve "place," unaware that often this hurt people already there. More significantly, many cities had become alarmingly dependent on Washington, looking there for guidance as well as resources. Some already appeared to be developing new kinds of autonomy and more self-reliance. In growing cities in the Sunbelt, this might be no surprise, but to also find it in the Northeast is more heartening. It seems particularly significant that Pittsburgh, which lost almost 30 percent of its population between 1960 and 1980, seems remarkably confident about its future. Officials in this city seemed well along in developing a sense of how to cope with local expectations, matching needs with resources.

In most cities, allocating federal funds was a visible and symbolic process, often triggering debates quite out of proportion to the impact such limited resources could actually make. Local officials often seemed compelled to disperse funds too broadly to have much effective impact, possibly afraid of the repercussions of targeting or charges of "triage." Yet there were examples of harmonious, even disinterested, citizen participation and of successful targeting without charges of discrimination or favoritism. Why couldn't city B do what city A did? Officials would only volunteer privately the constraints upon them. Broadly, the problem usually boiled down to reconciling unrealistic and often conflicting citizens' expectations with the limited things officials felt they actually could do.

The key to effective revitalization appears to lie in this local interplay between available resources and citizen expectations of government. If citizens "expect" grants yet enough grants cannot be provided, deviousness or conflict in the political arena increases. If, however, citizens can be required to earn access to below-market-rate loans *in ways the local ethos views as fair,* a more open, harmonious process results. Understanding what shapes this local ethos has now become very important. Obviously it is a complex process with many unidentified variables.

One shaper has clearly been Washington. When determining who should get favorable credit terms and how favorable those terms should be, the usual response of city officials has been to look to Washington, not only for more resources, but also for clarifying regulations. This has been a self-defeating move in the long run because Washington's criteria tended to raise expectations beyond the attainable. In effect, Washington simply promised everyone a decent, affordable home in a suitable neighborhood. It seems all HUD program guidelines were derived from this impossible goal. Yet federal officials avoided or could not state explicitly how and when this goal could actually be reached. The fact that HUD never completed its homework (or found sufficient funds) created countless, insoluble local problems.

The constructive response, ironically, is not to look to Washington. Local officials must come to understand the local situation more completely and concentrate on modifying what the local ethos views as fair. If there is not enough to go around, what can we do with what we have? Expectations can be tempered and influenced; available resources can both leverage more and be rationed as rewards rather than granted as a right. In any case, the gap between resources and expectations must be bridged.

Too often public resources intended for closing this gap actually widened it by displacing private efforts, whether the issue be jobs, housing, credit, or home insurance. The harder the public sector was striving to deliver, the more that private interests abdicated. Those who previously furnished most jobs, housing, credit, or insurance often retreated rather than join hands with government programs.

Many efforts, like establishing community development corporations, rehabilitating abandoned buildings, or putting together a UDAG, appear laudable when seen individually. Taken collectively, however, and viewed in broader perspective, the net impact of such efforts was frequently counterproductive; too often they also masked underlying problems, thereby curtailing further efforts to address them. Yet, those who contributed so much to these efforts also resist any process that puts them into context, or belittles their accomplishments.

The Reagan election can be interpreted as signaling that government resources are no longer available to be used unilaterally to bridge the local expectations gaps. Necessity now will force a good deal of rethinking on the part of all interests. Ultimately this is likely to be very healthy, but the short-term challenges loom as very traumatic. Local interests must now devise entirely new assistance roles, including revising expectations.

Before discussing what can be done about unrealistic expectations, it is worth mentioning what made them unrealistic. Many little-recognized forces recently altered the basic "lay of the land" for different areas, as discussed in chapter 2. Minor differences at the margin in employment, credit, and housing markets snowballed into national media images contrasting "boom" and "gloom." These are also underlying shapers of local ethos and expectations.

The media obscured important details in the basic lay of the land but they can also be a partner in fostering more realistic local expectations. Newspapers and television increasingly shape the local ethos by subtly influencing people's views of the world as they evaluate changes, problems, options, and progress toward solutions. In the early stages of the RAP study, *Dividing the Pie*, researchers subscribed to newspapers in each city. This proved to be an unexpectedly useful "window" onto what actually shaped local decision making. Initially, researchers expected the local papers to offer them only a preview of the reality to be encountered in each city, but it turned out that the media images were generally accepted locally as *the* reality.

Cities are simply too complex for most people to know about much more than what happens on their own corners. They allow the media to distinguish a fluke from a trend. Opinions and most actions on recent urban issues of which people are aware—redlining, gentrification, displacement, condominium conversion—have essentially been orchestrated through media coverage. Virtually every city has had its disastrous fire or hazardous spill that prompted hasty policy formulation after a spate of editorializing in the media.

In urban affairs, media images have often seemed more important than the events that actually occurred. Many a city official has recognized that how he is presented in the media is more important than what he does in person. Herein lies a problem. The media can project things as better or worse than they actually are. A poorly executed rehabilitation project with indefensible cost overruns can be presented as a major housing accomplishment, when time will reveal it as a housing disaster by any standard.

Skilled neighborhood groups in many cities have also learned that a good press image is a powerful tool to enhance their standing with public officials. Neighborhood press conferences are becoming key policy instruments, enabling shrewd neighborhood leaders to obtain major benefits for their constituents. However, this often seems quite unfair to other interests, and polarizes the local policy process. (This strategy is brilliantly described by Tom Wolfe in *Mau-mauing the Flak-Catchers*.)

Misusing the media or ignoring their influences, even unintentionally, can ultimately prove very harmful. As time reveals earlier misperceptions, mistrust grows. Raising unattainable expectations or portraying a false reality leads eventually to increased cynicism—this is a lesson of Vietnam come home to repeat itself in our neighborhoods.

The Reagan cutbacks now challenge local interests to become more resourceful. This requires developing a much deeper understanding of the local urban system and its context. Citizen expectations and the local ethos are important to consider in redefining a fair role for the public sector to play. Admittedly this redefinition will not be easy. Understanding the motivations shaping the actions of private and community interests is vital to a fresh start because these interests have so much to contribute and are not limited to their past roles of criticizing, confronting, or withdrawing. Developing this understanding involves placing less faith in Washington's guidance and avoiding "capture" by the media. Instead, it requires establishing a participatory process with the important interests. Those interests, in turn, then begin to help close the gap between currently identifiable resources and everyone's expectations by discovering overlooked resources and moderating expectations at the same time.

How does this increased local understanding come about? Once again, through developing the three-tiered information system and then following the checklist for reexamining governance presented in figure 5.1.

APPLYING ASSISTANCE MORE PRODUCTIVELY

Local officials may not yet believe that such a radical redefinition of local effort is called for, or how much more productive it can be. They may still be yearning for a continuation of the familiar, be it comprehensive planning or preparation of the type of submissions required by HUD in the past. In that case their actions in denying the new realities are part of the problem, wasting everyone's resources.

This chapter has outlined the way officials in some cities are devising their own approaches by reconsidering local context, expectations, and available resources. This is proving to be quite exciting; it is like discovering something previously overlooked: quality vintage housing and young, highly motivated home buyers.

In New Haven, Connecticut, people have devoted considerable time and effort in creating a citywide task force, including residents and aldermen along with private sector representatives and city staff. The task force started by monitoring neighborhood changes and attitudes and has since proposed a complete reformulation of the city's role in its neighborhoods.

Pittsburgh has perhaps the greatest head start in getting back on its feet after suffering much trauma, outmigration, and abandonment. The original Neighborhood Housing Services (NHS) concept, as well as effective rent escrowing, originated there. These are clearly useful prototypes for resolving the difficult questions posed by revitalization. In the past decade, Pittsburgh pioneered many urban initiatives. Each constructively links local private, public, and community interests in ways that define responsibilities and collectively result in tempering expectations while tapping hidden resources. This process of getting each actor to assume his proper role is well illustrated by NHS, proving it can be done in a city weakened by adverse economic and demographic trends.

As understanding of the local patterns increases, more can be achieved with less outside assistance. Local interests become more resourceful. Imaginative new approaches open up to handle difficult challenges like displacement, condominium conversions, and demands for controls on rents. In the past, these challenges were often framed by the media in ways that triggered counterproductive policies.

Municipalities may also begin to act jointly, redefining federal assistance guidelines or revising federal policies like the income tax code and credit system. These were indirectly but fundamentally reshaping U.S. housing during the last decade while local officials tried to administer HUD programs. The National League of Cities might join with the U.S. League of Savings and Loans to work also toward implementation of some basic federal changes like those discussed in chapter 4, as the mayors and bankers come to realize limited block grants cannot solve the problems facing today's urban residents.

The change of climate in Washington poses problems for those whose attention is still riveted there. Many local governments will doubtless continue to look there for more guidance and resources. However, the challenge ahead is to devise new ways of understanding the realities and perceptions in order to address today's complex neighborhood problems more effectively. These will involve a significant reassessment of the role of local government. The new roles include learning to recognize and deal with citizen expectations and neighborhood dynamics, developing more harmonious teamwork with other urban interests, citizens and private institutions, and turning to more imaginative uses of so-called governance techniques—before simply spending public monies.

Executive Summary
TWO SCENARIOS* 6

The election of President Reagan signals a transition. It is as if a curtain had been dropped, separating the next act from the New Deal/Great Society era with its ambitious but much contested social welfare programs.

The time is at hand for a return to basics in housing, to concentrate on matching supply to demand. Unexpected forces currently lock many into their housing. Upon moving, tenants face tough choices and sharp rent increases, and home owners must yield up their favorable mortgages. Already it is becoming clear that past assistance often obscured rather than helped the functioning of the market. Now, with little new development, housing pressures are becoming much greater, especially on the vulnerable poor and any new households that form or move.

This concluding chapter summarizes the current housing realities, stressing their volatility. Misleading perceptions increasingly shape counterproductive actions. Two contrasting scenarios are developed to illustrate the difference that solid policy analysis can make.

The laissez-faire scenario describes a future being shaped by current, myopic actions. With less government and few new initiatives, it shows that widespread housing revitalization will not be spontaneous. Without new assistance, the socioeconomic fabric will not mend—it may even tear apart.

The restructured housing incentives scenario, the alternative, summarizes the new approach called for by the analysis in this book. A broader

---

*Portions of this chapter appeared in a slightly different form in *Journal of Housing* (November/December 1982).

grasp of available resources and current housing dynamics will enable the many interests engaged in producing, maintaining, adapting, and converting housing to serve all more equitably and efficiently. In this scenario, feedback from current realities shapes new, more productive responses. These enhance the effectiveness of self-interests acting in local markets.

Many people will consider such a restructuring too drastic or politically impossible. However, examining housing issues from a fresh perspective reveals the inappropriateness of many past initiatives—and suggests the need for a whole new approach. Modifying home-owner deductions, providing housing vouchers to tenants and new savings incentives to home buyers may seem too radical; developing a new local intelligence for understanding and dealing with neighborhood dynamics may seem both unnecessary and costly. However, this analysis suggests that efforts in these new directions *will* play a significant role in the next act because they are cost-effective.

Admittedly, future actions in the housing drama are likely to require some compromises between these two scenarios. However, presenting these contrasts engages the reader to become more informed and join the upcoming debate, rather than to sit back, simply taking issue with "Reaganomic answers" to complex problems.

THE CURRENT REALITIES

The situation for those now with homes looks very different from the way it looks to those without them. Phenomenal appreciation and unaffordability capture the contrast. Even among renters, the perceptions of new home-seekers are poles apart from the views of those who remain rooted and have not moved in years. Today's realities also differ sharply from the conventional wisdom, drawn from a past that was never fully understood. Yet all these conflicting impressions currently drive housing actions. New information and understanding can improve the local matching of demand with supply.

In trying to settle down, the baby-boom generation has upset past demographic and housing market patterns nearly everywhere. Smaller households, especially a minority often childless and with two careers, promise to imprint housing patterns throughout the 1980s. Wherever housing shortages loom, values inflate, eroding the moderate income stock and providing windfalls to some prior owners.

Growth and adaptation of the stock to new demands are hampered, not only by astronomical financing costs, but often by zoning controls, unrealistic perceptions, and counterproductive regulations as well. An increasing share of new additions have been manufactured homes and unsanctioned conversions within existing structures. Single-family construction is giving way to cluster developments. New multifamily development is limited and increasingly going condo. The one household in three that still rents is becoming economically and spatially squeezed, yet the assisted inventory has virtually stopped growing. More subsidies will be required simply to preserve it for those already there.

For too many, the American dream home has now become unaffordable—to own, to heat, and to maintain properly, let alone to buy. The soaring appreciation that made single-family homes such an attractive tax shelter and inflation hedge during the 1970s rested on long-term fixed rate mortgages and baby-boom demand. This helped those already owning in the 1970s to gain handsomely, but it also diverted much capital away from more productive investments in private enterprise and industry.

To build or buy a home has now become so difficult that shelter ingenuity is already turning to adaptive reuse, to reconditioning old buildings and to carving out space for new households within the existing shelter envelope, turning "onesies into twosies."

Traditional rental housing is also in trouble as current capital costs enter upon turnover, compounding with soaring operating expenses. Much existing housing no longer pays its way. The housing focus promises to shift from new production toward recycling and revamping existing housing. Traditional construction is dwindling; home building has turned out to be as vulnerable as the auto industry. And the thrift industry is already altering beyond belief.

The story of the young couple that buy their dream house "with the old lady still inside"—she providing their financing directly while they provide her security—may still seem apocryphal to lenders and home-builders, but it aptly captures newly emerging approaches to both financing and communal responsibilities. Taking in boarders or becoming a landlord sounds like steps backward, but "home sharing," creating accessory apartments, and two households buying jointly as "mingles" are becoming accepted as new ways to shelter the one out of four households unsuited to conventional resident ownership.

THE LAISSEZ-FAIRE SCENARIO

As the housing bubble of the late 1970s threatens to burst, effective demand for more housing is sharply reduced. Trading up is much less attractive when mortgage rates are so far above the rate of inflation and indexed as well. Meanwhile, under laissez-faire, the rest of the market, particularly entering home buyers, are completely excluded by current home prices and financing costs. Only where carrying costs force builders to sell off already-built inventory are there any sales—and these are at steep discounts or "buy downs" often reducing nominal prices by 15 percent and more.

The home builders, fighting for survival, assail the Federal Reserve's tight credit policy. Along with potential home-buyers, they press on all fronts for "affordable," that is, reduced-interest mortgages.

Politicians attempt to tap pension funds for additional sources of housing credit to accompany expansion of tax-exempt bonds, unaware that hidden links in financial markets will soon raise the cost of these funds as well. At the same time provisions limiting pension fund proceeds to unionized construction will further inflate the cost of the resulting homes. Yet without new construction, demand pressures will cause conversion of more existing stock, increasing the hardships upon renters.

Lenders scramble for the new savings to be generated by tax-deferred IRA accounts while trying to forget the discouraging consumer response to their ads for tax-exempt All-Savers certificates. As underemployment, a stalled housing market, and high interest rates persist, most outstanding mortgage portfolios look worse and worse. They contain both newer, high-interest adjustable-rate mortgages beginning to show disconcerting default rates alongside well-seasoned, underwater mortgages that last and last, eating up the net worth of lenders every day they continue. Henceforth, lenders that survive will view themselves as loan servicers.

New, multifaceted money managers involving well-known firms like Sears, American Express, and Merrill Lynch move in from the wings. While weak banks are being merged into stronger ones, and FDIC estimates the catastrophic losses to be underwritten by the tax payers, the entire credit world is being shaken to its roots.

Real estate brokering, which used to be a genteel occupation open to suburban wives with spare time, becomes ruthlessly competitive, requiring computers to project creative financing alternatives and sensitivity training to handle the hopes and phobias of home buyers and sellers.

Authors, who used to brag about making millions in real estate, turn to "Creative Financing, All You Wish You Never Had to Know," rendering creative financing suspect.

Owner renovators and nonunion operators emerge as more important forces in the housing sector than major contractors who cannot employ their backhoes and union labor in refurbishing existing stock.

Local officials, lacking understanding of what keeps them in the frying pan, persist in committing dwindling public funds to construct award-winning but token assisted housing. The few elderly projects they complete, at $80,000 per unit, even include wheelchair ramps and grab bars. However, as tenant waiting lists and frustrations mount, local officials face near chaos in resident selection.

The bright and able quickly recognize that, despite the potential of revitalization, public office is no place to sit as explosive socioeconomic forces build up—leaving such posts to others, who in effect demand combat pay while making muddles worse.

This continuing turmoil enhances some already existing housing, attracting speculators. However, it also forces all actors into a make-do approach as many interests fight to survive. In the popular mind, urban revitalization and baby-boom demographics were heralded as remaking whole cities when in fact they touched only the most attractive portions. There, for windfall profits, private market processes often recondition stock that low-income families used to occupy.

In the absence of statistics, no one really knows where "displacees" go under laissez-faire. Somehow, they resemble those no longer listed as unemployed after their benefits ran out. Displacees drop out of the conscious housing system; there is only recognition that crime and abandonment remain problems. The underlying links between urban revitalization, doubling up, displacement, and poverty escape notice.

Nor is the very selective and fickle nature of the new urban housing demand commonly recognized: "Show me only this street with that house type. Over there? Not on your life!" Media reports of lurid crimes and rising insurance costs in the "gilded ghettoes" adjoining inner-city wastelands make property values increasingly volatile—and residents more nervous and defensive about *any* change.

The secondary market soon discovers that despite strong urban demand, too many housing loans are unsound; investors in mortgage-backed securities begin to shun mortgages on stock that could quickly go "out of fashion" or become exposed to vandalism and violence.

Those who already own their homes, the Haves, feel lucky and still claim to identify with those continuing to strive toward home ownership, despite acquisition costs requiring two careers and postponement of child raising. The Haves need new buyers to maintain housing demand despite high-interest mortgages. On the other hand, lower-class tenants are unwanted, seen as harbingers of changes like more welfare, poverty, and unemployment.

Debates heat up around measures like rent and eviction controls, accessory apartments, credit allocation, and condominium conversion rights. These engage the passions of a society no longer producing much housing under laissez-faire and instead polarizing into Haves and Have-Nots in fights about existing stock.

What Is Wrong with the Laissez-Faire Scenario?

The housing system just described functions wastefully, inefficiently, and inequitably. Poor information leads to fragmented efforts to cope with differences between individual interests. These in turn prevent individuals from seeing the broader picture or finding solid common ground. Realtors, lenders, builders, and sellers are exploring "creative financing" or mortgaging the future, rather than jointly seeking ways to reduce the rate of inflation in housing values to again make dwellings affordable. Values simply cannot remain long at more than four times resident incomes—particularly if the buyer must finance ownership at today's interest rates. Everything "wrong" with the current housing system cannot be summarized here. However, a few elements stand out.

Housing markets need more than a return to laissez-faire to work effectively. Basic mismatches between supply and demand in credit, as well as in housing, need to be addressed through better information. Shortsighted interventions often compounded problems, but they were pursued for good reasons. Lifting a few regulations, cutting some taxes, suspending most assistance for the disadvantaged, and hoping that pension funds coupled with creative financing can solve today's housing problems are not enough.

There is enough shelter space, overall, particularly when measured by European standards, but it is unevenly distributed and inefficiently owned, partly due to federal credit and tax policies, and partly due to local regulations. Since household growth will soon taper down in many areas, boosting traditional construction should not receive priority despite the hardships upon home builders. Just as inflation in housing values must be curbed, so must the "filter-down, throwaway, and abandon" mentality that has become unaffordable because it is so wasteful. However, some new housing models are needed.

The uneven distribution of existing housing has several facets worth distinguishing: intergenerational, interregional, and interclass inequities.

The intergenerational differences are the most profound, yet also the most obscured. Housing performance in the 1970s generated norms regarding home buying that were based on a double fluke: fixed interest rates compounded by baby-boom demographics. Even though these norms are very inappropriate to the 1980s, they will persist for some time. Today's home seekers need two incomes to buy because recent buyers, viewing homes as income tax shelter, bid values up excessively. In addition, today's buyers are asked to pay interest at well *over* the rate of inflation to make up for buyers in the 1970s who got away with paying below the rate of inflation.

Interregional factors operate at many scales ranging from national to local. An Ohio surplus does not help people who want homes in California; nor do suburban homes with good yards and schools help the two-career couple committed to city living. Because housing lasts so long and cannot be moved, policies must now influence demand as well as alter supply. Reshaping demand involves not only locating more jobs where people already are, but also changing living patterns, slowing the rate at which people move out on their own and getting people to live in nearby housing they had not previously considered. Conversions can alter the supply to serve more, smaller households. Skillful refurbishing can adapt old stock to these new demands. Here, local zoning must not stand in the way of appropriate new uses like accessory apartments being created in empty-nester singles.

The class bias toward the affluent is the thorniest issue to address. As the "pie of housing opportunities" stops expanding, competition increases. But credit terms favor the advantaged. A 13 percent mortgage still feels high to anyone taking only the standard tax deductions, but for someone in the 40 percent tax bracket, its effective rate after itemizing deductions drops to below 8 percent, probably below the future rate of inflation. The current tax code thereby fosters conversion of former rental housing to more affluent home ownership wherever demand is strong. This erosion of rental stock can displace poorer and elderly tenants as effectively as any bulldozer, even if the displacees remain anonymous.

Intergenerational inequities can be attributed to luck, both good and bad and thereby accepted. Dealing with national imbalances will require measures beyond housing policies. Interclass differences, however, require new tax and credit policies. The current federal tax bias toward the affluent buyer needs to be addressed to prevent flareup of class warfare wherever different classes compete for the same stock. Only then can local efforts to deal with demand/supply mismatches become effective. In all this, new construction, even in desired locations, can do far less than most people realize. American housing goals are undergoing transformation.

RESTRUCTURING HOUSING INCENTIVES: AN ALTERNATIVE SCENARIO

Modifying federal home-owner income tax deductions is the first federal policy change in this scenario to improve local housing markets. Converting them to a universal 25 percent tax credit and capping them at $3,000 help everyone more fairly toward resident ownership. This prevents shortages from inflating the value of existing housing as a collectible and slows conversion of lower-income rental stock to condominiums for the affluent. Since current home-owner deductions are estimated to increase by $10 billion every year (the Congressional Budget Office sees them reaching $50 billion by fiscal 1984), this also helps balance the budget.

Each home owner's housing costs (up to $12,000 per year in mortgage interest and property taxes) are thereby tax-exempted, even for those who take the standard deduction. This encourages median-priced development to continue. As those in higher tax brackets shift more investment toward enterprise and industry, this improves both housing equity and efficiency throughout the economy. As less resources remain tied up in mortgages of the affluent, the overall demand for housing credit also drops, reducing the general push on interest rates and easing inflation further. The CPI also levels off along with mortgage and acquisition costs for existing housing, slowing the rise in indexed federal transfer payments like social security and moderating wage demands throughout the economy.

Federal housing vouchers and a *savings for home-buying program* complement the tax restructuring. Section 8 has been discontinued because it undermined rather than preserved private rental housing, served only a fraction of the needy, and cost $6,000 annually per unit paid directly to some housing providers. Housing vouchers for low-income and elderly tenants are more suited to aiding them yet keeping the providers of rental housing in business. A housing voucher program providing households $3,000 annually ($250 per month including administration) costs $3 billion per million participating tenant households. Obviously this is much more than the Reagan administration's proposed housing payments concept, but that is the level of commitment required to preserve rental housing. Eventually this voucher program expands over three years to serve five million tenants, costing $15 billion annually.

A *savings for home-buying program* is created in this scenario by a new partnership between the lending industry and the federal government to help home buyers and builders as well as the lenders. In the first year $250 million in government premiums (plus tax shelter) starts half a million households, saving $2.5 billion for home ownership, averting the need for most bank bail-outs and mergers. In the second year this swells to over $8 billion in savings. In five years $1.5 billion in annual government home-savings premiums sustains a $44 billion savings pool providing half a million new home buyers with 10 percent mortgages every year.

Thrift institutions offer these tax-exempt savings accounts to future home buyers, adapting the German *Bausparkassen* concept and linking it with the rapid U.S. acceptance of Keogh and IRA tax-exempt savings plans, as elaborated in chapter 4. These accounts provide lenders a vital inflow of billions in savings in the next several years. As soon as individual households attain their savings target, they gain access to their accumulated savings, including interest and government premiums, for home purchase. Paying half the acquisition costs up front, they also obtain financing for the balance at below-market interest rates from funds that others who subsequently join the program are still depositing.

The above scenario illustrates a new federal three-pronged approach to housing policy. Modifying and capping home-owner tax expenditures to prevent their increasing by $10 billion every year, then translating the resulting savings into housing vouchers and federal incentives to reward more home savings together cost less than laissez-faire. The vouchers to save rental housing are the dominant new cost element, rising from some $5 billion in the first year to level off at a $15 billion annual level after five years. Policy makers could step up home-savings incentives through more subsidies and diminish rental vouchers to reflect a policy decision to phase out rental tenure. In any case, restructured housing assistance and tax expenditures still remain well below the costs of allowing laissez-faire patterns to continue.

Local actions in this scenario focus on improving market information and broadening everyone's understanding of the dynamic housing forces in order to fine-tune the effects of the federal changes. Objective research disseminated by some trustworthy, neutral agency like an "urban observatory" clarifies the underlying patterns in the complex local real estate system. In order to revise citizen expectations and reintroduce public assistance in more productive ways, local actions begin by monitoring neighborhood change and reexamining the incentives and barriers shaping the actions of all housing interests.

Since neighborhood housing markets now experience sharply diverging influences often leading to speculation alongside disinvestment, basic reeducation is essential for all policy interests, public, private, and community. Matching neighborhood housing supply to demand emerges as a critical but little recognized local responsibility.

An "observatory" monitoring changes on a parcel basis enables municipalities, institutions, and community groups to grasp neighborhood dynamics. Interests can then be influenced to stabilize local housing markets and countervail against dysfunctional practices. Since the late 1970s, market context data have been collected by individual lenders each time a home loan application was made, but these data have never been analyzed. They reflect the market climate surrounding each property at time of sale. Monitoring such data leads communities toward understanding the local real estate "weather changes," and to understand what actually shapes the local markets. This turns the art of monitoring neighborhood change into a useful science. No longer can one assume that change is caused principally by bankers, minorities, slumlords, too little federal aid, or any other convenient scapegoat. Tracking changes in market climate is more subtle and revealing than simply being current on sales prices. It enables communities to anticipate future trends and spend public resources more effectively.

How the Alternative Scenario Improves the Housing Market System

Demographics, new life-styles, energy scarcity are all difficult to alter, but the income tax code and credit system, as products of Congress, can now be constructively harnessed to reshape the housing system.

Such basic changes in federal policies affecting housing are long overdue, even if they seem as yet politically unlikely. To do less is mere tinkering, and to shift action to the state and local levels or the private sector without such changes (as the Reagan administration threatens to do) only continues to mask underlying problems.

Expectations now shape countless housing decisions to move or stay, sell or buy, invest or do nothing. Many neighborhood changes proceed from misleading perceptions that become self-fulfilling prophecies. To redirect housing actions wherever the urban fabric is coming under stress now requires understanding "governance" and dealing with the expectations already shaping the behavior of all the various housing interests. What motivates and constrains each one? How can behavior be beneficially altered through public policies? We must first understand what really shapes housing behavior instead of simply continuing to spend public resources in ways that conventional wisdom and the most vocal community leaders seem to direct.

Tenants fixing a leaking hot water faucet rather than idly cursing the landlord take a little but important first step toward improving their housing. They soon come to feel more self-reliant and less antagonistic. The household that stays and adds a room rather than moving out soon helps build a sense of community. Many such little changes coming together can begin to mend local housing systems.

Neighborhood Housing Services (NHS) originated in Pittsburgh from public discussions extending over years. These began with what bothered people and eventually reached the roots of housing behavior. Along with creating the basic NHS concept (which is now being federally propagated), the process improved code enforcement and local statutes covering rent delinquencies, established an effective housing court and clinic, and sanctioned and upgraded illicit marginal dwelling units that were little better than boarding rooms—and that was just in the beginning of what Pittsburgh has justifiably called its real "renaissance."

A "neighborhood listening" posture can generate suitable new concepts regarding home-sharing, accessory apartments, conversions, adaptive reuse, and appropriate new developments like congregate elderly housing. It can also guide regulatory decontrol, revising or eliminating counterproductive laws and practices like those governing zoning, controlling rents, evictions, and condo conversions, or setting priorities for obtaining federal assistance. As yet, most planning is very traditional, still preoccupied with responding to crises or conducted from ivory towers. If we put one-tenth the time, talent, and resources into understanding change that are spent responding to crises, our feelings about housing and then the housing itself will radically improve.

An entirely new approach can arise from neighborhood analyses, aided by Apple or Radio Shack interactive microcomputers, which not only temper expectations realistically, but reveal overlooked resources and more productive uses for public block grant assistance. This approach can also organize a constituency to bring about the required federal changes. This alternative approach may not be easy, but it is becoming necessary. To do less to improve neighborhood housing markets is ultimately futile.

For too long, it seems, the drone of the federal policy machinery lulled and obscured much already happening "by itself" in countless communities. Recently, this federal engine of urban revitalization produced more noise than power, promising but not really taking people where they want to go. Thus the defenders of Section 8 were few. Now the federal engine seems suddenly shut down. After the initial panic, communities are finding they are in their own small sailboats with only limited auxiliary power. With a better knowledge of weather, wind, and tides, they can still get where they choose; but now they must understand what is possible and decide their own destinations. Who knows, getting there may even become more enjoyable.

Notes

CHAPTER 1

1. Goetze (1977): iii.

CHAPTER 2

1. William C. Baer, "Empty Housing Space: An Overlooked Resource," quoted in Stokes (1981): 46.
2. See appendix A for the statistical base prepared by Cushing Dolbeare of the Low Income Housing Coalition from 1978 *AHS* data.
3. Lowry (1981): 25.
4. Congressional Budget Office (1981): 7, table 1.
5. Congressional Budget Office (1981): 9, table 2.
6. Poterba (1980).
7. Hendershott and Shilling (1980).

CHAPTER 3

1. Lowry (1981) cites the following: U.S. General Accounting Office (1979), *Rental Housing: A National Problem that Needs Immediate Attention*. Report to Congress by the Comptroller General, CED..80–11 (November 8) and the Pollyana Institute (1980), *Rental Housing: Two Decades of Progress*, Washington, D.C. The latter may be merely a device invented by Lowry.
2. Lowry (1981): 24.
3. Lowry (1981): 25.
4. Lowry (1981): 32.
5. Lauber (1981).

6. Goetze (1979), chapter 5, "Deriving a Housing Policy Law," details how owner types relate to changing market dynamics.
7. Lowry (1981): 35.
8. Corporation for Public Broadcasting (1981).
9. Stockard and Engler, Inc. (1981).
10. Goetze (1976) developed this conceptual framework in chapter 3, "Neighborhood Revitalization Strategies."
11. Public Affairs Counseling (1975).
12. Goetze and Colton (1980) detail ways to tailor strategies to local neighborhood dynamics.
13. Goetze (1979) chapter 7, "Media Images of Neighborhoods," elaborates how neighborhood housing demand can be influenced through media images.
14. Sorkin (1982), chapter 2, "Patterns of Neighborhood Change," summarizes the findings from the HUD-supported Research Triangle Institute (RTI) and National Institute for Advanced Studies (NIAS) investigations plus a dozen others on displacement research.
15. Pittsburgh Department of Housing (1981).
16. Boston Redevelopment Authority (1980): 122.
17. *New York Times*, November 30, 1981, p. 1.
18. The Conservation Foundation (1981) describes a host of such concepts.
19. Hare (1981): 33.
20. Hare (1981): 32–35.
21. Metropolitan Area Planning Council (1978).
22. Metropolitan Washington Council of Governments (1981). MWCOG surveyed 33 localities nationally that were thought to permit such dwellings. Twenty responded but, of these, 6 in fact did not permit them. Of the 14 that did, only 1 allowed them prior to 1970, and 5 only started in the last 18 months.
23. *New York Times*, December 8, 1981, p. 82, "A Suburban Tempest: Neighbors Riled by In-House Apartments."
24. U.S. Department of Housing and Urban Development (1980). The 1.3% statistic misleads Congress and the American public; HUD neither subtracted out public housing and rentals in 1–4's unsuited to conversion, nor elaborated on the way the conversions are concentrated in strong market pockets, not uniformly distributed nationally.
25. Grier and Grier (1981).
26. U.S. Congress (1981), Rosenthal hearings.
27. U.S. Congress (1981): 171.

CHAPTER 4

1. President's Commission on Housing (1981).
2. Goetze (1981b).
3. Frieden and Walter (1980).
4. Lowry (1971).
5. Frieden and Walter (1980).
6. Goetze (1981a).

7. Andreassi and MacRae (1979).
8. Personal interview with Dr. Ulrich Pfeiffer, West German housing minister, Bonn, October 5, 1981.

CHAPTER 5

1. Sorkin (1982) compares several land use information systems.
2. SRI-International (1980).
3. National League of Cities/U.S. Conference of Mayors (1973), "Better Communities Act: The Cities Speak," mimeo, (April).
4. Boston Neighborhood Development Agency (1980), *Dividing the Pie*. This study, funded by HUD through the Urban Consortium, explored resource allocation decisions affecting neighborhoods in twenty-eight major cities and eight urban counties.

Appendix A

HOUSING STOCK COMPOSITION BY TENURE AND INCOME, 1978

Table A presents data on households by annual income, units by monthly cost—all by tenure status. These statistics were derived from the Annual Housing Survey, volume C, table A 1 by the Low Income Housing Information Service.

Figure 2.1 shows the same data graphically to array the stock alongside the households. For over half of all renters, all those under $10,000, there is a serious shortage of affordable units. However only one-seventh of all owners with mortgages have incomes under $10,000, and for many of these housing remained affordable.

Many more owners under $10,000 are without mortgages altogether, and their housing costs appear quite reasonable.

TABLE A
Comparison of Households (by Income) and Units (by Monthly Cost) at 25% Cost–Income Ratio, U.S., 1978

(in thousands of households and units)

Households, by annual income/ units, by monthly cost	Renters	Owners, Mortgaged	Owners, Unmortgaged
Under $3,000 income	3,288	789	1,597
Under $62.50/month cost	1,647	119	2,951
Deficit/surplus	−1,641	− 670	+1,354
$3,000–6,999 income	6,723	1,714	4,404
$62.50–145.81 cost	5,625	1,132	10,471
Deficit/surplus	−1,098	− 582	+6,067

$7,000–9,999 income	4,361	2,027	2,587
$145.81–208.31 cost	7,423	4,498	3,213
Deficit/surplus	+3,062	+2,471	+ 626
$10,000–14,999 income	5,748	5,274	3,454
$208.33–312.48 cost	8,933	10,452	1,204
Deficit/surplus	3,185	5,178	−2,250
$15,000–19,999 income	3,174	5,745	2,071
$312.48–416.64 cost	2,273	7,489	214
Deficit/surplus	− 901	1,744	−1,857
$20,000–24,999 income	1,816	5,773	1,498
$416.64–510.81 cost	622	4,076	67
Deficit/surplus	−1,194	−1,697	−1,431
$25,000–34,999 income	1,225	6,283	1,469
$510.81–729.14 cost	297	3,269	25
Deficit/surplus	− 928	−3,014	−1,444
$35,000–49,000 income	379	2,931	658
$729.14–1,041.64 cost	42	794	8
Deficit/surplus	− 337	−2,137	− 650
$50,000 or more income	170	1,589	421
$1,041.66 or more cost	23	297	5
Deficit/surplus	− 147	−1,292	− 416
TOTAL	26,884	32,125	18,158
	34.8%	41.6%	23.5%

SOURCE: Derived from 1978 *Annual Housing Survey,* vol. C, table A-1. Gross Rent includes utilities; owner costs include principal, interest, taxes, insurance, and utilities. Prepared by, and reprinted with the permission of, Low Income Housing Information Service.

Appendix B

FEDERALLY CHARTERED AGENCIES AND DIRECT EXPENDITURE PROGRAMS THAT PROMOTE HOME OWNERSHIP*

In addition to the tax benefits the federal government charters and, in some cases, funds through direct expenditures a number of agencies that promote home ownership. Some of these agencies provide loan guarantees and other services so that home buyers can obtain more favorable mortgage loans. Others regulate and expand the supply of funds for home mortgage lending. Six of these agencies and their programs are described briefly in this appendix: the Federal Housing Administration (FHA), the Veterans Administration (VA), the Federal Home Loan Bank System (FHLBS), the privately owned Federal National Mortgage Association (FNMA), the Government National Mortgage Association (GNMA), and the Federal Home Loan Mortgage Corporation (FHLMC).

LOAN GUARANTEES AND RELATED SERVICES

The federal government funds two major insurance activities to provide home buyers with more favorable mortgage loans: the mortgage insurance and graduated payment mortgage programs of the Federal Housing Administration (FHA) and the mortgage guarantee and direct loan programs of the Veterans Administration (VA).

Federal Housing Administration (FHA)

The Federal Housing Administration (FHA), founded in 1934, provides a number of services designed to promote home ownership. The best

*Adapted from Congressional Budget Office (1981).

known of these is the FHA mortgage insurance program, a self-financing activity under which the federal government guarantees 100 percent of all qualifying mortgage loans in return for a lender's offering certain lending terms favorable to borrowers. Another FHA activity that has gained prominence recently is its promotion of graduated payment loans through the Section 245 program.

In recent years, the share of FHA-insured home mortgages has declined significantly, to between 10 and 15 percent of all new home mortgages, because of the growth of private mortgage insurance and the gradual acceptance of low-down-payment, long-term-amortized mortgage loans. During fiscal year 1981, the FHA is authorized to commit nearly $34.2 billion in mortgage loan guarantees.

Veterans Administration (VA)

Since the enactment of the GI Bill following World War II, loan guarantees and direct mortgage loans have been among the most popular services offered by the Veterans Administration. VA loan guarantees are normally limited to the lesser of 60 percent of the mortgage or a specified dollar amount, now set at $27,500. Because the guarantee normally exceeds the loss from foreclosure for all except relatively expensive homes, many VA loans require little or no down payment. During fiscal year 1981, the VA is expected to guarantee an estimated $10.5 billion worth of new home mortgage loans. For fiscal year 1982, the total is expected to reach $11.2 billion.

REGULATION AND EXPANSION OF MORTGAGE LENDING

Four other federally sponsored organizations serve to regulate and expand the volume of home mortgage lending in the United States: the Federal Home Loan Bank System (FHLBS), the Federal National Mortgage Association (FNMA), the Government National Mortgage Association (GNMA), and the Federal Home Loan Mortgage Corporation (FHLMC). Each of these institutions promotes these objectives in a somewhat different way.

Federal Home Loan Bank System (FHLBS)

The Federal Home Loan Bank System (FHLBS), consisting of a Federal Home Loan Bank Board (FHLBB) and 12 regional home loan banks, performs many of the same activities for federally insured savings and loan (S&L) associations that the Federal Reserve System undertakes for commercial banks. The FHLBS monitors savings and loan activities, advancing money to S&Ls in need of additional funds. The FHLBB regulates all savings and loan deposit and lending activities of federally insured S&Ls. Thus, it determines what types of loans and deposits S&Ls may offer.

Federal National Mortgage Association (FNMA)

The Federal National Mortgage Association (FNMA), founded in 1938 and made a private corporation in 1968, is the oldest of the federally sponsored agencies providing additional funds for mortgage lending through the creation of a "secondary market" for mortgage loans. FNMA has traditionally served as a mortgage dealer, alternatively buying and selling mortgages to maintain the liquidity of the home mortgage market. Since the mid-1960s, however, FNMA has been required to purchase certain types of mortgages involving low- and moderate-income home buyers, thus becoming a net holder of home mortgages. Although FNMA is authorized to borrow some funds from the federal government, its activities have thus far been financed solely by the sale of its own bonds.

Government National Mortgage Association (GNMA)

The Government National Mortgage Association (GNMA) was created in 1968 to assume some of the more specialized duties originally assigned to FNMA. Thus far, GNMA has performed two major tasks. One is to expand the secondary mortgage market by creating a new type of federally insured security, the GNMA mortgage-backed security. The other has been to subsidize mortgage lenders, by purchasing below-market-rate mortgages at par and selling them at market value—what is called the GNMA "Tandem" plan. GNMA's Tandem activities are supported directly by federal appropriation; its mortgage-backed security activities are self-financing. In fiscal year 1981, GNMA is expected to increase its net commitments of mortgages by about $650 million, while its guarantees for mortgage-backed securities are authorized to reach $53 billion. The income from this last activity is expected to exceed expenses by about $89.4 million.

Federal Home Loan Mortgage Corporation (FHLMC)

The Federal Home Loan Mortgage Corporation (FHLMC) is the newest of the federal mortgage assistance agencies. It serves to purchase mortgages directly from mortgage originators, primarily savings and loan associations. Founded in 1970, FHLMC has acquired over $27.3 billion in mortgages and other loans receivable. Like FNMA and GNMA, it supports its activities by raising funds through the sale of low-rate federal bonds. FHLMC stock is owned by the regional home loan banks of the Federal Home Loan Bank System.

Appendix C

RECENT INNOVATIONS IN HOME MORTGAGE INSTRUMENTS*

Significant changes in home financing have occurred in the last several years. In place of the traditional, level-payment, fixed-interest-rate mortgage, lenders and home buyers have increasingly opted for a number of different mortgage instruments. Some of these provide lenders more protection against unexpected fluctuations in interest rates by allowing changes in the mortgage rate itself and corresponding alterations in monthly payments. Others permit buyers to afford more expensive homes by allowing mortgage payments to rise over the term of the loan in place of the constant, level payment. Still other mortgages allow home buyers to reduce their monthly mortgage payments by giving lenders part of the increase in the value of their homes when they are later sold or after a specified time. Each of these new mortgage instruments represents a market response to the effects of inflation on house prices and interest rates. Nevertheless, certain obstacles may limit the spread of these new instruments. Following is a brief discussion of the major innovations in home mortgage finance and their potential hazards.[1]

---

*Adapted from Congressional Budget Office (1981).
Reproduced from the Congressional Budget Office (1981), The Tax Treatment of Homeownership: Issues and Options, pp. 71–73.
Reproduced from the Congressional Budget Office (1981), The Tax Treatment of Home ownership: Issues and Options," pp. 75–77.

1. For more extended discussions of new mortgage instruments, see Rochelle L. Stanfield, "High Interest Rates are Sparking a Revolution in Home Financing," *National Journal*, vol. 13 (January 31, 1981), pp. 172–76; and Federal Home Loan Bank Board, *Alternative Mortgage Instruments Study* (November 1977).

MAJOR NEW INSTRUMENTS AND THEIR HAZARDS

Of the many new mortgage instruments that have become prominent during the last several years, the limited-adjustment variable rate mortgage (VRM), the renegotiable rate mortgage (RRM), the graduated payment mortgage (GPM), and the shared appreciation mortgage (SAM) have received the most attention. In addition to these three new instruments, the Federal Home Loan Bank Board (FHLBB) has recently liberalized mortgage lending rules for federally insured savings and loan associations. Under these rules, S&Ls can now make 40-year mortgage loans with down payments as low, in some cases, as 5 percent.[2]

Limited-adjustment "variable rate mortgages" are mortgages in which interest rates and monthly payments may change, based on changes in a predetermined index such as the Treasury bill rate, but not beyond certain limits. Under some mortgages of this type, the interest rate may only change by a limited amount during any time period; for example, some loans prohibit interest rate changes of more than ½ percentage point during any 12 months. Some loans also limit the total possible change in interest rates over the term of the mortgage. Other variable rate mortgages allow unlimited changes in interest rates but restrict changes in monthly payments to certain frequencies, such as every several years. Under one such plan, monthly payments remain fixed for five years, but any shortfall of payments from true obligations is used to increase the loan balance. This increase in the loan balance, called "negative amortization," is then used to determine the new set of monthly payments at the end of that five-year period.[3]

While variable rate mortgages protect lenders against interest rate fluctuations, they pass that risk on to borrowers. Many consumer groups have thus objected to VRMs, although likely consumer reactions to them will depend on economic conditions and the range of financing options available.

Renegotiable rate mortgages (RRMs) are another type of mortgage that allows interest rates to change during the term of the loan. With these loans, the lender can renegotiate the interest rate and monthly payments to reflect current conditions at specified intervals. Like VRMs, they let lenders offset the higher cost of funds when interest rates rise and the yields on long-term mortgages fall below current market levels. Their major difference from VRMs is that interest rates are changed only when the loan comes up

---

2. See "Revision of Real Estate Lending Regulations," *Federal Register*, vol. 45 (November 18, 1980), pp. 76096 ff., esp. pp. 76096–97 and 76099, affecting 12 CFR §545.6.
3. See "Buyers Adrift: How Floating Rates Affect More Home Purchasers," *Wall Street Journal* (May 6, 1981), pp. 1, 20.

for renegotiation. Like VRMs, RRMs have also been criticized by some consumer groups. In addition, some lenders have had to offer them at a discount to attract borrowers.[4]

Graduated payment mortgages (GPMs), pioneered by the U.S. Department of Housing and Urban Development (HUD) through the Section 245 housing program, are loans in which payments begin below the level of full amortization and then rise during the first several years until they reach a level where the balance can be fully paid by the end of the loan term. While payments are rising, the loan balance increases; this represents the negative amortization discussed earlier. These types of instruments can allow young families with prospects for income growth to afford larger mortgages than they otherwise might. They can create problems, however, if family incomes do not grow as anticipated. In addition, they provide lenders with greater risk and lower returns than do conventional mortgages at the same interest rate, because the negative amortization can be taxed even though no cash payments are received.

Shared appreciation mortgages (SAMs), the newest of the alternative mortgage instruments, provide borrowers with below-market interest costs in return for giving the lender a percentage of any increase in the price of a home. Under one type of SAM, borrowers receive a one-third reduction in interest rates in return for allowing the lender a one-third share in any rise in housing value at the date of sale or during the first ten years of ownership. This type of loan may prove advantageous to home owners expecting large income gains or small increases in house prices. It can pose problems, however, if house price appreciation greatly exceeds the rise in the borrower's income. In addition, some critics fear it could lead to "redlining," because lenders would favor more affluent neighborhoods with greater chances of house price appreciation.[5]

---

4. See "Business Struggles to Market the RRM," *Savings and Loan News*, vol. 110 (July 1980), pp. 30–34.
5. See Kenneth R. Harney, "Criticized SAM Loans in Limbo," *Washington Post* (January 10, 1981), p. F10; and Stanfield, "High Interest Rates," p. 174. Lenders who did redline could incur penalties under the Community Reinvestment Act of 1977, 12 U.S.C. §§29012905 (1977).

Bibliography

Andreassi, Michael W., and Duncan MacRae. 1979. *Metropolitan Housing and the Income Tax*. Washington, D.C.: The Urban Institute (July).

Boston Neighborhood Development Agency. 1980. *Dividing the Pie: Resource Allocation to Urban Neighborhoods*. Boston, Mass.

Boston Redevelopment Authority. 1980. *Boston's Housing in the 1980s: Challenges and Opportunities*. Boston, Mass. (September).

Congressional Budget Office. 1981. *The Tax Treatment of Homeownership: Issues and Options*. Washington, D.C. (September).

The Conservation Foundation. 1981. *Aging in City Places: A Sourcebook of Ideas to Help the Elderly in Revitalizing Neighborhoods*. Washington, D.C.

Corporation for Public Broadcasting. 1981. *U.S. Chronicle: Downward Mobility* (broadcast November 16).

Downs, Anthony. 1980. "Too much Capital for Housing?" *Brookings Bulletin*. Vol. 17, no. 1. Washington, D.C.: Brookings Institution.

Frieden, Bernard J., and Adrian Ruth Walter. 1980. *What Have We Learned from the Housing Allowance Experiment?* Cambridge, Mass.: Joint Center for Urban Studies of MIT and Harvard University.

Goetze, Rolf. 1976. *Building Neighborhood Confidence: A Humanistic Strategy for Urban Housing*. Cambridge, Mass.: Ballinger Publishing Company.

Goetze, Rolf. 1979. *Understanding Neighborhood Change: The Role of Expectations in Urban Revitalization*. Cambridge, Mass.: Ballinger Publishing Company.

Goetze, Rolf. 1980. "Federal Tax Expenditures Should Be Restructured to Aid Urban Housing." *Journal of Housing* 37, no. 9 (October): 504–512.

Goetze, Rolf. 1981a. "The Housing Bubble." *Working Papers for a Democratic Society* (January–February): 44–52.

Goetze, Rolf. 1981b. "The Impact of National Tax Policies on Rental Housing." In *Federal Income Tax Policies and Housing*, edited by Gary Hack, pp. 1–18. Cambridge, Mass.: Lincoln Institute of Land Policy. Monograph no. 81-9.

Goetze, Rolf, and Kent Colton. 1980. "The Dynamics of Neighborhoods: A Fresh Approach to Understanding Housing and Neighborhood Change." *AIP Journal* (April): 184–194.

Goetze, Rolf; Kent W. Colton; and Vincent F. O'Donnell. 1977. *Stabilizing Neighborhoods: A Fresh Approach to Housing Dynamics and Perceptions*. Boston, Mass.: Boston Redevelopment Authority (November).

Grier, George, and Eunice Grier. 1981. "Displacement: Where Things Stand." A Report to the Ford Foundation (February).

Hack, Gary, ed. 1981. *Federal Income Tax Policies and Housing*. Cambridge, Mass.: Lincoln Institute for Land Policy. Monograph No. 81-9.

Hare, Patrick H. 1981a. "Carving Up the American Dream." *Planning*. (July): 14–17.

Hare, Patrick H. 1981b. "Rethinking Single-Family Zoning: Growing Old in American Neighborhoods." *New England Journal of Human Services*. (Summer): 32–35.

Hendershott, Patric H., and Sheng Cheng Hu. 1979. *Inflation and the Benefits of Owner-Occupied Housing*. Cambridge, Mass.: National Bureau of Economic Research. Working Paper no. 383.

Hendershott, Patric H., and Kevin E. Villani. 1977. *Regulation and Reform of the Housing Finance System*. Washington, D.C.: American Enterprise Institute for Public Policy Research.

Hendershott, Patric H., and James D. Shilling. 1980. "The Economics of Tenure Choice, 1955–79." In *Research in Real Estate*, edited by C. F. Sirmans, vol. 1. JAI Press.

Johnson, M. Bruce. 1981. "Is the Sun Setting on the American Dream?" *Reason* (November): 37–40, 50.

Johnson, Warren. 1979. *Muddling Toward Frugality: A Blueprint for Survival in the 1980s*. Boulder, Colo.: Shambhala.

Kolodny, Robert. 1981. *Multi-Family Housing: Treating the Existing Stock*. Washington, D.C.: National Association of Housing and Redevelopment Officials.

Lauber, Daniel. 1981. "Condo Conversion Laws: The Next Generation." *Planning* (February): 19–23.

Lowry, Ira S. 1971. "Housing Assistance for Low-Income Families: A Fresh

Approach." U.S. Congress, House Committee on Banking and Currency. *Papers Submitted to Subcommittee on Housing Panels.* 92 Congress, 1st Session; Part 2: 489–523.

Lowry, Ira S. 1981. "Rental Housing in the 1970s: Searching for the Crisis." In *Rental Housing: Is There a Crisis?*, edited by John C. Weicher; Kevin E. Villani; and Elizabeth A. Roistacher. pp. 23–38. Washington, D.C.: The Urban Institute.

Metropolitan Area Planning Council. 1978. *Regulation of Accessory Apartments in the Metropolitan Boston Region.* Boston, Mass. (July).

Metropolitan Washington Council of Governments. 1981. *Accessory Apartments: A Local Housing Alternative.* Housing Technical Report No. 1981-4. (September). Washington, D.C.

Noto, Nonna A., 1980. *Tax Expenditures: The Link between Economic Intent and the Distribution of Benefits among High, Middle and Low Income Groups.* Congressional Research Service, Economics Division. Report No. 80–99E. (May).

Nutt-Powell, Thomas E. 1982. *Manufactured Homes.* Boston, Mass.: Auburn House Publishing Company.

Pittsburgh Department of Housing. 1981. *Housing: A Four Year Report.* Pittsburgh, Pa.

Poterba, James M. 1980. *Inflation, Income Taxes and Owner-Occupied Housing.* Cambridge, Mass.: National Bureau of Economic Research. Working Paper No. 553. (September).

President's Commission of Housing. 1981. *Interim Report.* Washington, D.C. (October).

President's Commission on Housing. 1982. *Financing the Housing Needs of the 1980s: A Preliminary Report on Housing Finance.* Washington, D.C. (January).

Public Affairs Counseling. 1975. *The Dynamics of Neighborhood Change.* Prepared for Office of Policy Development and Research of the U.S. Department of Housing and Urban Development. HUD-PDR–108(2).

Rosen, Harvey S. 1979. "Housing Decisions and the U.S. Income Tax." *Journal of Public Economics 11*, no. 1: 1–23.

Rosen, Harvey S., and Kenneth T. Rosen. 1980. "Federal Taxes and Homeownership: "Evidence from Time Series." *Journal of Political Economy 88*, No. 7: 59–75 (February).

Sternlieb, George, and James W. Hughes. 1981. *The Future of Rental Housing.* Rutgers University: Center for Urban Policy Research.

Stockard and Engler, Inc. 1981. *Housing and Neighborhoods: A Report to the Mayor's Housing Task Force, New Haven, Conn.* Chapter 1. Cambridge, Mass. (January).

Stokes, Bruce. 1981. *Global Housing Prospects: The Resource Constraints.*

Washington, D.C.: Worldwatch Institute, Paper no. 46. (September).
Turner, John F. C. 1977. *Housing By People: Towards Autonomy in Building Environments*. New York: Pantheon Books.
Turner, John F. C., and Robert Fichter., ed. 1972. *Freedom to Build: Dweller Control of the Housing Process*. New York: Macmillan.
Sorkin, Donna. 1982. *Yardsticks for Assessing Displacement and Neighborhood Change: A Report of the Local Government Review Panel on Displacement Research*. Washington, D.C.: Public Technology, Inc.
SRI-International. 1980. *Rediscovering Governance: Using Non-Service Approaches to Address Neighborhood Problems* Menlo Park, Calif. (February).
U.S. Congress. 1981. *Condominium and Cooperative Conversion: The Federal Response*. House Committee on Government Operations, Hearings before a Subcommittee. 97 Congress, 1st session. Part 1—Overview Hearings.
U.S. Department of Housing and Urban Development. 1980. *The Conversion of Rental Housing to Condominiums and Cooperatives: A National Study of Scope, Causes, and Impacts*. Washington, D.C.
H. C. Wainwright and Company. 1980. "Inflation, Taxes and the Affordability of Housing." *Economics*. Boston, Mass. (January 7).
Weicher, John C.; Kevin E. Villani; and Elizabeth A. Roistacher. eds. 1981. *Rental Housing: Is There a Crisis?* Washington, D.C.: Urban Institute Press.

SUBSCRIPTION PERIODICALS

Banker and Tradesman. Massachusetts' Real Estate, Banking and Commercial Weekly. Boston, Mass.
New York Times. New York.
Tax Angles. A Monthly Letter of Tax Saving Ideas, Strategies, Techniques. Alexandria, Virginia.
U.S. Housing Markets. Advance Mortgage Corporation. Detroit, Mich.

Index

Accelerated depreciation, 38, 41
  rehabilitation encouraged by, 7
Accessory apartments, 8, 46, 73–76, 117
  amount of, 13–14
  governance and, 109
  granny flats, 8, 73
Acquisition costs, 38, 40
All-Savers certificates, 92
Amortization, negative, 138
Annual Housing Survey (AHS)
  housing stock changes from, 11–14
  mobility, tenures, and housing costs from, 14–16
Apartments. See Rental housing
Appreciation, 117
  housing value inflation and, 30
Ashmont Hill, 71
Assisted and rental housing. See Rental housing

Baby boom, housing demand and, 4, 17, 54, 120
Balloon note, sales by, 22–23
Baltimore, public housing in, 84
Bausparkassen, 21, 96, 97, 122
Block grants. See Community Development Block Grants
Blue collar workers
  employment, 4
  as multifamily housing investors, 56
Boosterism, 71
Boston
  accessory apartments in, 75, 76
  boosting neighborhood confidence in, 71
  neighborhood change monitored in, 104
  public housing in, 79, 80–83
  weatherization of houses in, 72
Boston Urban Rehabilitation Program (BURP), 81
Boston's Housing Court (BHC), public housing and, 82
Brooke amendment, 82
"Buy downs", 23

California
  housing market in, 16, 18
  tenants' rights in, 50
Canada, mortgage system in, 20
Capital gains, Economic Recovery Tax Act and, 91
Census analysis, neighborhood dynamics studied with, 103
Class. See Income class
Cluster developments, 116
Community Development Block Grants (CDBG), 7, 24, 26, 38, 89–90, 109, 110
Community Reinvestment Act, 19
Computers. See Microcomputers
Condominiums, conversion to, 5, 35–36, 37, 40, 49, 52, 76–79, 87
  demand for, 10
  Department of Housing and Urban Development and, 77–78
  displacement and, 77, 78, 79
  housing value inflation and, 30
  moderate income, 51
  "Mom and Pop", 78
  number of, 11–12
  residual tenants and, 49–52, 59, 79
  in rising market, 69
  scarcity and, 77, 78
Conference on the Rental Housing Crisis, 44
"Consumer-oriented housing assistance grants", 90
Cooperatives
  limiting equity in, 51
  number of, 11–12
  see also Condominiums, conversion to
"Creative financing", mortgages and, 22, 91
Credit
  pension funds for, 90
  trends in, 18–23
  see also Mortgages
Credit for home buying program. See Home savings system

Declining neighborhood, housing in, 68–69

145

Demographics, regional shifts in housing demand due to changes in, 16–18
Denver, Land Use Information System in, 102
Department of Housing and Urban Development (HUD), 19
  citizen expectations and, 111
  condominium conversion and, 77–78
  limited equity cooperatives and, 51
  public housing and, 81, 82
  rental assistance and, 24
  units subsidized by, 26
Detroit, housing market in, 17
Developers, of multifamily housing, 55, 57
Development
  federally assisted, 7
  marketing the transfer rights of, 50
  opposition to new, 9
  private, 36
  as public and assisted housing. *See* Rental housing
Disintermediation, 19
Disinvestment, rental housing and, 55–57, 59
Displacement
  condominium conversions and, 77, 78, 79
  governance reconsideration and, 108–9
  in rental housing, 59
Distressed property handlers, 55, 57
Dividing the Pie: A Guide to Local Resource Allocation Practices, 110, 112
Downward mobility, 61

Economic Recovery Tax Act of 1981, 31, 77, 91–92
Elderly, 49
  accessory apartments for, 8, 51, 74–75, 76
  condominium conversion process and, 77, 78
  in private rental housing, 49, 53
  in public and assisted housing, 83, 86
  in suburbs, 74–75
Employment
  blue collar, 4
  regional shifts in demographics and, 17–18
  white collar, 4
Energy conservation, weatherization and, 61, 71–73, 87
England
  enterprise zones in, 108
  mortgage system in, 21
Enterprise zones, in England, 108
Excess capacity, in rental housing, 45, 54–55
Experimental Housing Assistance Project (EHAP), 93

Factory-built housing, 13
Federal government
  agencies promoting home ownership, 133–35
  changes in role of, 7–9
  citizen expectations and, 14
  Community Development Block Grants, 7, 24, 26, 38, 89–90, 109, 110
  Economic Recovery Tax Act of 1981 and, 31, 77, 91–92
  mortgage credit alterations and, 90–91
  public and assisted housing and. *See* Rental housing
  savings program for home buyers to be created by, 95–98, 122
  tax expenditure revision and, 91–92, 94–95
  voucher system, 39, 79, 89, 90, 93–94, 122–23
  see also Department of Housing and Urban Development; Homeowner deductions; Section 8 housing assistance programs
Federal Home Loan Bank Board (FHLBB), 134, 135, 138
Federal Home Loan Bank System (FHLBS), 134–35
Federal Home Loan Mortgage Corporation (FHLMC), 135
  Residential Appraisal Report Form 70, 63, 64–65, 67
Federal Housing Administration (FHA), 19–20, 133–35
Federal National Mortgage Association (FNMA), 19, 20, 135
  Residential Appraisal Report Form 70, 63, 64–65, 67
Filtration theory, 20, 36, 43, 60, 61
Fixed-interest mortgage, 4–5, 10, 18–19, 20, 90–91
Ford, Gerald, 7, 8
France, mortgage system in, 21

Gentrification, 9, 19, 50, 71, 78
Germany, *Bausparkassen* in, 21, 96, 97, 122
Governance, local government reexamining, 106–9
Government. *See* Federal government; Local government

Index

Government National Mortgage Association (GNMA), 135
Graduated payment mortgage (GPM), 22, 139
Grandfathering, existing tenants and, 50
Granny flats, 8, 73
Greenlining, 19

Hand-me-down theory, 36. *See also* Filtration theory
Heating costs
  public housing and, 80
  weatherization and, 61, 71–73, 87
Home-owner tax deductions, 9, 14, 24–25, 26, 29–36, 41, 49
  capping, 94–95, 121–22
  Economic Recovery Tax Act and, 91–92
  inflation and, 29–30, 31, 35
Home savings system, 95–98, 122
Home sharing, 51, 117. *See also* Accessory apartments
Housing Act of 1949, 23
Housing allowances. *See* Voucher system
Housing bonds, tax-exempt, 20
Housing costs
  acquisition costs and, 38, 40
  Annual Housing Survey of, 14–16
  operating costs and, 40–41
  Reagan and, 24
  tax-inflation interaction and, 35
  unaffordability and, 36–38
Housing Improvement Program, 109
Housing starts, 11, 12–13
Housing stock, *Annual Housing Survey* of, 11–14
Housing vouchers. *See* Voucher system
Houston, housing market in, 17

Income class, uneven distribution of housing and, 121. *See also* Lower income households; Upper income households
Indexed mortgages, 6
Individual Housing Accounts, 96
Individual Retirement Account (IRA), 21, 89, 92, 95, 97
Inflation
  home-owner deductions and, 29–30, 31, 35
  housing demand and, 4–5
  lack of mobility due to, 6
Interest rates
  fixed-interest mortgages and, 4–5, 10, 18–19, 20, 90–91

Regulation Q and, 19, 21
Intergenerational differences, uneven distribution of housing and, 120, 121
Investor types, multifamily housing and, 55, 56–57
Invsco, 78

J-51 tax abatements, 49

Keogh account, 89, 92, 95

Laissez-faire housing scenario, 115, 117–21
Land Use Information System, 102
Life tenure, existing tenants and, 50
Limited-adjustment variable rate mortgage (VRM), 21, 22, 138
Limiting equity, cooperatives and, 51
Lincoln Institute of Land Policy (LILP), 106
Local government
  citizen expectations and, 109–13
  governance reevaluation, 106–9
  media and, 112–13
  neighborhood change monitored by, 66, 102–6, 123, 124
  role reevaluation, 113–14
Lower-income households
  demand for housing by, 10
  as renters, 45–46

Macrohousing model, tax-inflation interactions and, 35
Massachusetts Housing Finance Agency (MHFA), 82
Media, local expectations and, 112–13
Metropolitan Area Planning Council (MAPC), 75
Metropolitan Washington Council of Governments (MWCOG), 75–76
Microareas, neighborhood dynamics studied by analyzing, 104–6
Microcomputers, neighborhood dynamics monitored with, 103–4, 105–6, 124–25
Mini-homes, 87
Mobile homes, number of, 11, 12–13
Mobility
  Annual Housing Survey of, 14
  downward, 61
  mortgages and lack of, 6
  resident-owned homes and, 6, 14, 60–61
  upward, 60
Mom and Pop condominium converters, 78

Money-market funds, 20, 21
Mortgage revenue bonds, 90
Mortgages
  balloon note for sales by elderly, 22–23
  buy downs, 23
  creative financing and, 22, 91
  escalation, 5
  federal government agencies promoting, 133–35
  fixed-interest, 4–5, 10, 18–19, 20, 90–91
  graduated payment, 22, 134
  housing units with and without, 14, 16, 131–32
  indexed, 6
  lack of mobility due to, 6
  redlining, 19
  renegotiable rate, 21, 22, 138–39
  reverse, 23
  secondary market in, 19–20, 21, 22
  shared appreciation, 22, 139
  thrift institutions providing, 18–19
  variable rate, 21, 22, 138
  wrap around, 22
  see also Home-owner tax deductions
Mother-in-law apartments. *See* Accessory apartments
Moving
  affordability of, 40
  decline in tendency, 5–6
  see also Mobility
Multifamily housing. *See* Condominiums, conversion to; Rental housing
Municipal Automated Geographic Information System (MAGIS), 102
Municipalities. *See* Local government

National League of Cities, 114
Negative amortization, 138
Neighborhood dynamics, 123
  confidence in neighborhood and, 71
  declining areas, 68–69
  demand for housing and, 61–67
  microcomputers for, 103–4, 105–6, 124–25
  monitoring, 102–6, 123, 124
  neighborhood listening, 104, 124
  public policy strategies for, 69–70
  rising areas, 69
  stable areas, 68
Neighborhood Housing Services (NHS), 113–14, 108, 124

Neighborhood listening, 104, 124
Neighborhoods
  changing. *See* Neighborhood dynamics
  housing demand and, 61–67
  media used by groups in, 112
Neighborhoods for Living, 71
New Haven
  citywide task force in, 113
  neighborhood listening in, 104, 124
New homes, number of, 11, 12–13
New York, J-51 tax abatements and, 49

Oakland, grandfathering rights of existing tenants in, 50
Office of Management and Budget (OMB), housing assistance and, 90
Ohio, housing market in, 18
Operating costs, 37, 38
  assisted and public housing, 79, 80
  rentals and, 40–41
Operators, of multifamily housing, 55, 56–57

Parcel-based system, neighborhood dynamics studied with, 103–4
Park Slope, 71
Pension funds, as housing credit, 90
Pittsburgh
  confidence in future in, 110
  Neighborhood Housing Services in, 113–14, 124
Pollyana report, 44–45
Population composition, regional shifts in housing demand due to changes in, 16–18
President's Commission on Housing (PCH), 90, 92, 93, 94
Private multifamily rental housing. *See* Rental housing
Property values, appreciation of, 10
Public housing. *See* Rental housing

Queens Village, 71

RAP study. *See Dividing the Pie: A Guide to Local Resource Allocation Practices*
Reagan, Ronald, 115
  Economic Recovery Tax Act and, 91–92
  housing assistance and, 7–8, 89–90
  housing costs and, 24
  local expectations and, 111, 113

Redlining, 19, 48
  shared appreciation mortgages and, 139
Regional shifts
  housing supply and demand and, 16–18
  uneven distribution of housing and, 120–21
Regulation Q, 19, 21
Rehabilitation, 47
  accelerated depreciation encouraging, 7
  of multifamily housing, 55, 57
Renegotiable-rate mortgages (RRMs), 21, 22, 138–39
Rent control, 39, 50
Rent vouchers. *See* Voucher system
Rental housing, 11, 14, 40, 42
  amount of lower cost, 14–16
  costs of, 37, 38, 40–41, 42, 117
  Economic Recovery Tax Act and, 91
  home-owner deductions limitation as benefit to, 94–95
  housing allowances and, 39
  number of, 11, 12–13
  private, 87. *See also* Condominiums, conversion to
  cooperatives, 51
  disinvestment and local policy, 55–57, 59
  displacement, 59
  efficient use of under-utilized space in, 51
  elderly tenants in, 49, 53
  excess capacity in, 45, 54
  grandfathering rights of tenants in, 50
  life tenure to tenants in, 50
  local policy on, 54–60
  lower-income households in, 45–46
  marketing transfer of development rights and, 50
  new tenure forms available for, 50–51
  overbuilding, 47–48
  ownership turnover reduction, 52–53, 59
  ownership types, 55, 56–57, 59
  red tape clarification and, 53
  rent control, 39, 50
  rent inadequacy, 46–49
  residual tenants rights in, 49–52, 59, 79
  revitalization, 49–50
  slumlords of, 53, 55, 59, 80
  speculation and local policy on, 55–57, 59
  in suburbs, 13
  vacancy rate, 45
  valuation, 46
  public and assisted, 23–29, 38–39, 79–86, 87. *See also* Section 8 housing assistance programs
    in Boston, 80–83
    Community Development Block Grants and, 7, 24, 26, 38, 89–90, 109, 110
    cutbacks in, 89–90
    for elderly, 83, 86
    heating problems, 80
    operating costs and, 79, 80, 85
    President's Commission on Housing and, 90, 92, 93, 94
    resistance to, 85–86
    reviving enthusiasm in, 83–86
    voucher system for, 39, 79, 89, 90, 93–94, 122–23
  taxation and, 25
Rental Housing: A National Problem that Needs Immediate Attention (1979), 44
Rental Housing: Two Decades of Progress (1980), 44–45
Rents, inadequacy of, 46–49
Residential Appraisal Report: FHLMC Form 70, 63, 64–65, 67
Resident-owned homes
  Ecomomic Recovery Tax Act and, 91
  energy conservation applied to, 71–73
  federal agencies promoting, 133–35
  housing costs and, 60–61
  by income and units, 131–32
  mobility and, 6, 14, 60–61
  mobility decline and, 60–61
  number of, 13
  restoration programs, 70
  reutilization of older homes, 61
  savings program for, 95–98, 122
  suburban, 13
  surplus in, 46
  tax credit for, 95
  unaffordability, 117
  see also Accessory apartments; Housing costs; Mortgages; Neighborhood dynamics; Suburbs
Restoration program, for resident-owned housing, 70
Restructured housing incentives, scenario on, 115–16, 121–25
Retirement
  Economic Recovery Tax Act and, 92
  Individual Retirement Account and, 21, 89,

150 RESCUING THE AMERICAN DREAM

92, 95, 97
Keoghs and, 89, 92, 95
trading up in housing and, 92
Reverse equity annuities, 23
Reverse mortgages, 23
Revitalization, 36
   citizen expectations and, 109–13
   redirecting neighborhood, 107–8
   of rental housing, 49–50
Rising neighborhoods, housing in, 69
Row-houses, 87

San Francisco
   grandfathering rights of existing tenants in, 50
   strong housing markets in, 16
Savings for home-buying program, 95–98, 122
Secondary market, for mortgages, 19–20, 21, 22
Section 8 housing assistance programs, 7, 8, 24, 38–39, 54, 80, 84, 85, 89–90, 93, 106, 125
   Boston housing and, 81–82
   displacement and, 109
   three-in-one, 81
Section 236, 85
Shared appreciation mortgages (SAMs), 22, 139
Shareholders, of multifamily housing, 55, 57
Single-family dwellings. *See* Resident-owned homes
Slumlords, 53, 55, 59, 80
Society Hill, 71
Speculation, 55–57, 59
   condominium conversion and, 77
   tax provisions causing, 9
SRI-International, 106, 107–8
Stable neighborhoods, housing in, 68
Stacked flats, 87
Suburbs
   demand for, 17, 41, 52
   elderly in, 74–75
   overbuilding in, 47–48
   private rental housing in, 13
Sunbelt, 62, 101, 110
Tandem plan (GNMA's), 135
Taxation
   Economic Recovery Tax Act and, 31, 77, 91–92
   rental units and, 25

sheltering and, 4, 10, 25, 92, 120
tax-credit for home owners and, 95. *See also* Home-owner tax deductions
"Tax bracket creep", 31
Tax credit, for home-owner, 95
Tax-exempt housing bonds, 20
Tax shelters, homes as, 4, 10, 25, 92, 120
Tenure, *Annual Housing Survey* of, 14–16. *See also* Mobility
Traders, of multifamily housing, 55, 56
Treasury bills, 19

Unaffordability, 116–17
Underutilization, 8–9, 51. *See also* Accessory apartments
Unsanctioned income units. *See* Accessory apartments
Upper income households. *See* Home-owner tax deductions
Upward mobility, 60
Urban Development Action Grants (UDAG), 26, 89–90
Urban renewal, 10, 35–36
   Department of Housing and Urban Development and, 19
   government involvement in, 19–20
   overbuilding and, 47–48
   reuse of existing structures in, 36

Variable rate mortgages (VRMs), 21, 22, 138
Veterans Administration (VA), 134
Voucher system, 39, 79, 89, 90, 93–94, 122–23

Washington, D.C.
   accessory apartments in, 75
   Municipal Automated Geographic Information System and, 102
   strong housing market in, 16
Weatherization, 61, 71–73, 87
White collar employment, 4
Windfall mortgage. *See* Fixed interest mortgage
Wrap around mortgage, 22

Zoning
   accessory apartments and home sharing and, 74, 109
   resident-owned homes and, 87